John 1–11

Son of God

JOHN A. STEWART

Lamplighters International is a Christian ministry that helps individuals engage with God and His Word and equips believers to be disciple-makers.

For additional information about Lamplighters ministry resources, contact:

Lamplighters International
771 NE Harding Street, Suite 250
Minneapolis, MN USA 55413
or visit our website at
www.LamplightersUSA.org.

Product Code Jn1-NK-2P

ISBN 978-1-931372-57-2

CONTENTS

How to Use This Study

What Is Lamplighters?

Lamplighters International is an evangelical Christian ministry that publishes Christ-centered, Bible-based curriculum and trains believers to be intentional disciple makers. This Bible study, comprising twelve individual lessons, is a self-contained unit and an integral part of the entire discipleship ministry. When you have completed the study, you will have a much greater understanding of a portion of God's Word, with many new truths that you can apply to your life.

How to study a Lamplighters Lesson

A Lamplighters study begins with prayer, your Bible, the weekly lesson, and a sincere desire to learn more about God's Word. The questions are presented in a progressive sequence as you work through the study material. You should not use Bible commentaries or other reference books (except a dictionary) until you have completed your weekly lesson and met with your weekly group. Approaching the Bible study in this way allows you to personally encounter many valuable spiritual truths from the Word of God.

To gain the most out of the Bible study, find a quiet place to complete your weekly lesson. Each lesson will take approximately 45–60 minutes to complete. You will likely spend more time on the first few lessons until you are familiar with the format, and our prayer is that each week will bring the discovery of important life principles.

The writing space within the weekly studies provides the opportunity for you to answer questions and respond to what you have learned. Putting answers in your own words, and including Scripture references where appropriate, will help you personalize and commit to memory the truths you have learned. The answers to the questions will be found in the Scripture references at the end of each question or in the passages listed at the beginning of each lesson.

If you are part of a small group, it's a good idea to record the specific dates that you'll be meeting to do the individual lessons. Record the specific dates each time the group will be meeting next to the lesson titles on the Contents page. Additional lines have been provided for you to record when you go through this same study at a later date.

The side margins in the lessons can be used for the spiritual insights you glean from other group or class members. Recording these spiritual truths will likely be a spiritual help to you and others when you go through this study again in the future.

AUDIO INTRODUCTION

A brief audio introduction is available to help you learn about the historical background of the book, gain an understanding of its theme and structure, and be introduced to some of the major truths. Audio introductions are available for all Lamplighters studies and are a great resource for the group leader; they can also be used to introduce the study to your group. To access the audio introductions, go to www.LamplightersUSA.org.

"DO YOU THINK?" QUESTIONS

Each weekly study has a few "do you think?" questions designed to help you to make personal applications from the biblical truths you are learning. In the first lesson the "do you think?" questions are placed in italic print for easy identification. If you are part of a study group, your insightful answers to these questions could be a great source of spiritual encouragement to others.

PERSONAL QUESTIONS

Occasionally you'll be asked to respond to personal questions. If you are part of a study group you may choose not to share your answers to these questions with the others. However, be sure to answer them for your own benefit because they will help you compare your present level of spiritual maturity to the biblical principles presented in the lesson.

A FINAL WORD

Throughout this study the masculine pronouns are frequently used in the generic sense to avoid awkward sentence construction. When the pronouns he, him, and his are used in reference to the Trinity (God the Father, Jesus Christ, and the Holy Spirit), they always refer to the masculine gender.

This Lamplighters study was written after many hours of careful preparation. It is our prayer that it will help you "… grow in the grace and knowledge of our Lord and Savior Jesus Christ. To Him be the glory both now and forever. Amen" (2 Peter 3:18).

What Is an Intentional Discipleship Bible Study?
The *Next Step* in Bible Study

The Lamplighters Bible study series is ideal for individual, small group, and classroom use. This Bible study is also designed for Intentional Discipleship training. An Intentional Discipleship (ID) Bible study has four key components. Individually they are not unique, but together they form the powerful core of the ID Bible study process.

1. Objective: Lamplighters is a discipleship training ministry that has a dual objective: (1) to help individuals engage with God and His Word and (2) to equip believers to be disciple-makers. The small group format provides extensive opportunity for ministry training, and it's not limited by facilities, finances, or a lack of leadership staffing.

2. Content: The Bible is the focus rather than Christian books. Answers to the study questions are included within the study guides, so the theology is in the study material, not in the leader's mind. This accomplishes two key objectives: (1) It gives the group leader confidence to lead another individual or small group without fear, and (2) it protects the small group from theological error.

3. Process: The ID Bible study process begins with an Open House, which is followed by a 6–14-week study, which is followed by a presentation of the Final Exam (see graphic on page 8). This process provides a natural environment for continuous spiritual growth and leadership development.

4. Leadership Development: As group participants grow in Christ, they naturally invite others to the groups. The leader-trainer (1) identifies and recruits new potential leaders from within the group, (2) helps them register for online discipleship training, and (3) provides in-class leadership mentoring until they are both competent and confident to lead a group according to the ID Bible study process. This leadership development process is scalable, progressive, and comprehensive.

Overview of the Leadership Training and Development Process

There are three stages of leadership training in the Intentional Discipleship process: (1) leading studies, (2) training leaders, and (3) multiplying groups (see appendix for greater detail).

Intentional Discipleship
Training & Development Process

3. Multiplying Groups
The "5 Steps" for Starting New Groups
The Audio Training Library (ATL)
The Importance of the Open House

1. Leading Studies
ST-A-R-T
10 Commandments
Solving All Group Problems

Open House

Basic Training (1x Per Year)

Final Exam

6-14 Week Study

2. Training Leaders
Four-fold ministry of a leader
The Three Diagnostic Questions
The 2P's for recruiting new leaders
The three stages of leadership training

How Can I Be Trained?

Included within this Bible study is the student workbook for Level 1 (Basic Training). Level 1 training is both free and optional. Level 1 training teaches you a simple 4-step process (ST-A-R-T) to help you prepare a life-changing Bible study and 10 proven small group leadership principles that will help your group thrive. To register for a Level 1 online training event, either as an individual or as a small group, go to www.LamplightersUSA.org/training or www.discipleUSA. org. If you have additional questions, you can also call 800-507-9516.

INTRODUCTION

For many people John is the most beloved book of the Bible and, for some, it's the first book they ever read in God's Word. John is a book that reads easily, and Jesus' extended interactions with individuals—Nicodemus (John 3), the woman at the well (John 4), Martha and Mary (John 11), and His disciples (John 13–17)—draw readers into the narrative and help them identify with biblical characters. Its easy style and compelling content have endeared John's gospel to millions of people throughout the centuries.

But don't think of John's gospel as simplistic or redundant—a sort of retelling of the other three Gospel stories. John also contains much information about Jesus Christ that's found nowhere else in the Bible. In fact, ninety-three percent of the material in John isn't found in any of the other gospels (*The Bible Knowledge Commentary*, vol. 2, p. 269). John's gospel has much to offer those who are new to the study of God's Word. In addition, for serious scholars and theologians, its rich Christology—the study of the person and work of Jesus Christ—challenges their deepest thoughts. Greek scholar A. T. Robertson described John as "the profoundest book in the Bible." The gospel of John is a book for all people and all ages.

BACKGROUND

In the strictest sense the authors of the four Gospels are anonymous. The author of John's gospel identifies himself only as "the disciple whom Jesus loved" (John 21:20). Based upon the book's internal evidence and external testimony (cf. Eusebius, *The Ecclesiastical History* 3.24.1), most conservative Bible scholars believe the apostle John wrote the gospel at Ephesus between AD 85 and 95.

FOUR GOSPELS OR ONE?

The question "Why are there four Gospels?" was best answered by first-century Christian theologian Origen, who said, "There are not four Gospels, but a fourfold Gospel." The four Gospels contain God's complete revelation of Jesus' earthly life and ministry.

Each gospel emphasizes a distinct aspect of Jesus' ministry: Matthew presents Jesus as Israel's promised Messiah (the *King of Israel*) and the fulfillment of God's covenants (or promises) to Abraham and David; Mark describes Jesus as the *Suffering Servant* of God; Luke depicts Jesus as the perfect man and rejected *Son of Man* whose compassion extended to all peoples; while John provides the vision of Jesus as the *Divine Son of God*.

THEME

No book in the Bible contains a more clearly stated purpose than John's gospel. In John 20:30–31, the apostle indicated that he had recorded certain "signs" so that readers would believe in Jesus as the Christ. The original evangelistic purpose of John's gospel continues to be fulfilled today as readers come to a saving faith in Jesus Christ as their Lord and Savior.

DISTINCTIVE FEATURES

① *A Book of Signs:* John's gospel has been called the "Book of Signs" because it contains seven divinely chosen signs (Greek *semeion*) that reveal the glory of God and Christ as the Son of God.

② *The "I am" Statements:* The book of John also contains seven "I am" statements (6:35; 8:12; 10:7; 10:11, 14; 11:25; 14:6; 15:1). Jesus' use of the important "I am" phrase presents an indisputable claim to His deity by mirroring God the Father's response to Moses when he was called to deliver the Israelites out of Egypt. When Moses asked God how he should reply when the Israelites asked who had sent him, God told Moses to say, "I AM has sent me to you" (Exodus 3:14). The four Hebrew consonants that are translated "I AM" in our English Bibles are known as the tetragrammaton. Out of reverence for God, no orthodox Jew would have used that phrase. Jesus' use of such sacred words was an obvious and undeniable claim to deity and a blasphemous statement to Jews (John 8:58; cf. verses 48, 53, and 59).

③ *The Call to Believe:* Another distinguishing characteristic of John's gospel is the frequent use of the word "believe" (Gk. *pisteuo*). The Greek verb (found 98 times in John's gospel) is most frequently found in the present tense, signifying continuous, active trust in Jesus. The use of this particular form provides strong evidence that true saving faith is not simply an *"I prayed the (salvation) prayer"* event that is void of any lasting genuine belief, but an abiding faith in Jesus Christ as Savior and Lord that leads to a life of dedication to Jesus Christ and authentic worship of God.

④ *The Use of Mashal:* The apostle John records Jesus' frequent use of a Hebrew form of speech known as *mashal*. A mashal is an enigmatic and paradoxical saying that contains both a pointed and a veiled remark, often in the form of a riddle: for example, "Destroy this temple, and in three days I will raise it up" (John 2:19). Mashals create "communications obstacles" for those who are prideful and self-righteous but stimulate curiosity and spiritual interest in the hearts of those being drawn to God.

11

ONE

IS JESUS REALLY GOD?

Read Introduction, John 1:1–18; other references as given.

John 1:1–18 forms the introduction (or prologue) to the fourth gospel. In this passage the apostle John introduces us to a number of key words and phrases that dominate the remainder of the book: *witness*, *Word*, *life*, *light*, *darkness*, *belief*, and *truth*.

It is here that we're also introduced to another John. John the Baptist was a transitional figure between the Old and New Testaments and a mighty witness for Christ. Like the Old Testament prophets before him, John the Baptist preached a powerful message of repentance. Like the New Testament apostles and prophets, he bore witness to Jesus as the promised Messiah and the sinless Son of God.

Before you begin, please ask God to reveal Himself through His Word and to give you grace to accept the truths you will be learning.

1. The gospels of Matthew, Mark, and Luke begin with a bold declaration that Jesus is God, but John's gospel begins with a powerful theological statement in the form of a riddle. Rather than simply telling us who Jesus is, John invites his readers to discover Jesus' true identity for themselves.

   a. What *do you think* are the three most common opinions about who Jesus Christ was or is?

   _____

Lombardi Time Rule:

If the leader arrives early, he or she has time to pray, prepare the room, and greet others personally.

———

ADD GROUP INSIGHTS BELOW

_____

_____

_____

b. Who *do you think* Jesus was or is, and why?

_____

_____

_____

2. If you are somewhat familiar with the Bible, likely you realize that the first words of John 1:1 (**In the beginning was the Word**) are similar to the first words in the Bible (Genesis 1:1, **In the beginning God**).

a. Genesis 1 describes the new *physical creation*; John's gospel describes the new *spiritual* creation (life in Christ). In both verses the phrase **in the beginning** refers to the same event. To what event or time *do you think* it refers?

_____

_____

_____

b. John 1:1 says **In the beginning was**, not "in the beginning *is*." What or who was in existence before "the beginning" (Genesis 1:1–2; John 1:1)?

_____

_____

3. Use of the term *Word* in John 1:1 may seem strange to you. To Greeks (non-Jews or Gentiles), *word* meant not only the spoken word but also the thought (or reasoning of the mind) before the words were spoken. To the Hebrews, *Word* meant God's revelation to man (cf. Genesis 15:1, **The Word of the Lord came to Abram**). John's use of the term *Word* (John 1:1, Gk. *logos*) was uniquely powerful, meaning "ultimate

reason" to the Greeks and "ultimate revelation" (from God) to the Jews.

a. To this point in our study the true identity of the **Word** has not been disclosed. List at least four important truths the Bible teaches about the **Word** (John 1:1–3).

_____

_____

_____

_____

_____

_____

b. Which words and phrases are used to emphasize that all creation is the direct result of the Word's creative power, rather than evolution or a by-product of chance such as the "Big Bang" theory (John 1:3, 10; Colossians 1:16)?

_____

_____

_____

_____

4. The best commentary (or interpretative aid) on the Bible is the Bible itself. Use the following verses to determine the exact identity of the **Word** in John 1:1–3, and support your interpretation with specific verse references (John 1:1, 2, 14, 17).

_____

_____

_____

_____

_____

Want to learn how to lead a life-changing Bible study or start another study? Go to www.LamplightersUSA.org/training to learn how.

ADDITIONAL INSIGHTS

5. What *do you think* is the meaning of the phrase **In Him was life** (John 1:4)?

    _____

    _____

    _____

    _____

    _____

6. Some Christians don't seem to believe that **the light shines in the darkness** (John 1:5). Rather than believing that God's light (truth) overcomes the darkness (sin) of this world, they live and speak as if the darkness is an unstoppable force that irresistibly overwhelms the light of God's truth. If Christians don't grasp the truth of God's power over sin, they could be tempted to (1) withdraw from the world (isolation), (2) allow themselves to be assimilated into the world (worldliness), or (3) live in defeat and complain about the advancement of wickedness in society (including state schools and government).

    a. If you are a Christian, do you truly believe that the light (of Christ) shines in the darkness, and the darkness cannot overcome it (Holman Christian Standard Bible), or do you believe the darkness overcomes the light?

        _____

        _____

    b. Are you living in spiritual defeat, overcome by fear and forsaking biblical responsibilities to be a witness for Christ? Or are you living in the light, experiencing victory in Christ and boldly spreading the message of Christ to those in spiritual darkness?

        _____

        _____

c. What specific things could you do to let Christ's light shine through you more brightly at home ... at work... in your church ... in your community?

_____

_____

7. John the Baptist was a mighty servant of God. Jesus said, **among those born of women there is not a greater prophet than John the Baptist** (Luke 7:28).

a. What was the sole purpose of John the Baptist's life (John 1:6–8)?

_____

_____

_____

b. Just before Jesus ascended into heaven (Acts 1:9–11), He commanded His followers to be His witnesses (Acts 1:8). In what way do you think John the Baptist's ministry and a New Testament Christian's ministry are similar?

_____

_____

_____

_____

8. a. Jesus came into the world He created (John 1:3; Colossians 1:16), but those He created rejected Him (John 1:10–11). On what basis does a person become a child of God (John 1:12–13)?

_____

_____

_____

_____

If you use table tents or name tags, it will help visitors feel more comfortable and new members will be assimilated more easily into your group.

———

ADDITIONAL INSIGHTS

b. List three common misconceptions (false beliefs that are unacceptable to God [John 1:13]) many people believe about how they can enter heaven.

_____

_____

_____

_____

_____

_____

9. Most Christians tend to live lives that are either truth-based or grace-based. Those who conduct themselves strictly based on truth often lack grace in their lives. Those who rely heavily on grace often lack the spiritual courage to stand up for the truth. Jesus, however, was *full* **of grace and truth** (John 1:14, emphasis added). What do you think that means?

_____

_____

_____

_____

_____

_____

_____

_____

TWO

BEHOLD, THE LAMB!

Read John 1:19–51;
other references as given.

The prologue to John's gospel (1:1–18) begins with an introduction of Jesus as the Word of God and concludes with a summary statement that Jesus Christ is the declaration of God (John 1:18).

Jesus Christ is God! He existed before time began, and He is the creator of all things (John 1:1–3). Jesus came to those He created, but His own people did not accept Him (John 1:10–11). **But as many as received Him, to them He gave the right to become children of God** (John 1:12).

This second lesson focuses on (1) John the Baptist's testimony of Jesus as the Christ, and (2) the initial call of two of John's followers to be Jesus' original disciples. In John's interaction with religious leaders, you will see a profound example of true humility.

Before you begin, please ask God to reveal Himself through His Word and to give you grace to accept the truths you will be learning.

Zip It Rule:

Group members should agree to disagree, but should never be disagreeable.

ADD GROUP INSIGHTS BELOW

1. Andrew Murray, the late South African pastor and writer, said, "Humility is not a Christian grace like the other graces. It is the foundation of all Christian graces."

   a. What do you think are characteristics of a truly humble person?

   _____

_____

_____

_____

b. **God resists the proud, but gives grace to the humble**
(James 4:6). In what areas of your life do you continue
to see pride manifesting itself?

_____

_____

_____

2. John the Baptist's ministry was so powerful that the Jewish
religious leaders sent representatives to question him about
his true identity (John 1:19–27).

a. When the Jewish priests and Levites questioned John,
what specific things did he say to point them to Christ
rather than draw attention to himself (John 1:19–27)?

_____

_____

_____

_____

_____

b. Elijah was an Old Testament prophet who died hundreds
of years earlier. Why did the Jewish priests and Levites
ask John if he was Elijah (John 1:21; Malachi 4:4–6;
Matthew 11:7–14)?

_____

_____

_____

c. Since Jesus said John the Baptist was Elijah who is to

come (Matthew 11:11-15), why did John deny it (John 1:21)?

_____

_____

_____

3. In your own words, identify an important spiritual truth from each of the following verses to help you become a more humble person.

a. Psalm 24:1. _____

_____

b. Mark 10:44–45. _____

_____

c. John 15:5. _____

_____

d. 1 Corinthians 4:7._____

_____

e. 2 Corinthians 10:17. _____

_____

f. James 4:10. _____

_____

4. John the Baptist called Jesus **the Lamb of God** (John 1:29, 36), an obvious reference to the Passover lamb that God instructed the Israelites to sacrifice on the night they left Egypt (Exodus 12).

a. What happened at the time of the original Passover observance when the Jews placed the lamb's blood on the doorposts and the lintels (main support piece over the doors) of their homes (Exodus 12:1–7, 21–23)?

_____

b. The Passover lamb had to be **without blemish** (Exodus 12:5; NIV: "without defect"), meaning the sacrificed animal must be free of physical defects. No maimed, injured, or disfigured animal was an acceptable sacrifice to God. What important statement did the writer of Hebrews include in Hebrews 9:14 that identified Christ's sacrifice on the cross with the Old Testament Passover lamb and John the Baptist's statement that Jesus was the Lamb of God?

_____

5. In his natural state, man is unacceptable to a holy God because he is not **without blemish** (without sin, Romans 3:10–12). There is nothing you can do (good works, religious acts, gifts of charity, etc.) to abrogate or nullify your sinful condition. Do you believe you are a sinner incapable of saving yourself from eternal judgment by your own good religious or moral efforts? If you would like to know how you can be saved from God's judgment, turn to "The Final Exam" at the back of this book.

_____

_____

_____

6. John's statement **I did not know Him** is mentioned twice to emphasize that the baptizer did not originally comprehend Jesus' true identity (John 1:31, 33). Who did John eventually understand Jesus to be (John 1:29–34)?

_____

_____

_____

7. Jesus called two of John's followers to be His original disciples (John 1:35–40). When Andrew and an unnamed individual (likely the apostle John) began to follow Jesus, He turned and said, **What do you seek?** (John 1:38; NIV: "What

do you want?"). Some Bible commentators understand Jesus' question to mean "What are you really seeking in a relationship with me?"

a. What types of things do people desire from God (Mark 3:2; Luke 11:29; John 6:26–27)?

_____

_____

_____

_____

b. What did the God-fearing Greeks ask Philip (John 12:20–21)?

_____

_____

c. Honestly evaluate your relationship with God. What is the *main* thing you are seeking from a relationship with Him?

_____

_____

8. a. Whom did Andrew tell his brother Peter he had found (John 1:41)?

_____

b. Whom did Philip tell Nathaniel he had found (John 1:45)?

_____

_____

c. Whom did Nathaniel believe Jesus to be (John 1:49)?

_____

_____

9. When Jesus said to Nathaniel **Behold, an Israelite indeed, in whom is no deceit!** (John 1:47), He used a play on words in order to contrast Nathaniel's honorable character to the Old Testament patriarch Jacob (also known as Israel), who was a deceiver. Jacob had two powerful encounters with God—the first being a dream of angels ascending and descending on a ladder to and from heaven (Genesis 28:10–17). Jesus' use of this illustration would have been very familiar to Nathaniel. Carefully study Genesis 28:10–17 and John 1:50–51. What important addition does Jesus make to Jacob's original dream, and what do you think it signifies?

    _____

    _____

10. List ten words or phrases (and their corresponding verse references) used to describe Jesus in John 1.

    _____

    _____

    _____

    _____

    _____

    _____

    _____

    _____

    _____

    _____

THREE

THE FIRST
MIRACULOUS SIGN

Read John 2;
other references as given.

In the first chapter of John, the apostle helped readers discover the true identity of Jesus as the Christ (John 1:1–18). He also introduced us to John the Baptist, who testified that Jesus is the Lamb of God (John 1:19–34). At this point Jesus called His first five disciples: Andrew, an unnamed disciple (likely John), Peter, Philip, and Nathaniel.

This lesson focuses on two firsts: Jesus' first miraculous sign (John 2:1–12), and the cleansing of the temple in Jerusalem (John 2:13–25).

Before you begin, please ask God to reveal Himself through His Word and to give you grace to accept the truths you will be learning.

Volunteer Rule:

If the leader asks for volunteers to read, pray, and answer the questions, group members will be more inclined to invite newcomers.

ADD GROUP
INSIGHTS BELOW

1. In John 2:1 the opening words **On the third day** may seem confusing. Looking back to John 1:29, 35, and 43, four days had already been identified, and the stage appeared set for "On the fifth day." John's use of the phrase **On the third day**, however, was intentional, highlighting a very important event that had occurred two days earlier. What was that event (John 1:35–39)?

    _____

    _____

    _____

_____

_____

2. Ancient Near East weddings usually were elaborate events that routinely lasted an entire week. Virgins were married on Wednesdays, and widows were married on Thursdays. The bridegroom and bride would enter into a formal betrothal agreement before the groom left to prepare their new home prior to the wedding. A betrothal was somewhat similar to a modern engagement, except that it was legally binding and dissolvable only by divorce (Matthew 1:18–19). The actual wedding began when the groom and his friends went in the evening to the bride's home in a torchlight procession. The couple then proceeded to the wedding, where the festivities would begin. The wedding host (master of the feast; John 2:8) was responsible for making sure food and beverages were available for the entire wedding event. Any host who failed to do so could have been held legally responsible.

a. Jesus and His disciples were invited to this particular wedding. Author Warren Wiersbe says, "It is a wise couple who invites Jesus to their wedding." Do you think Mary's statement about the lack of wine (John 2:3–4) was a simple observation, or was it an implied appeal for Jesus to solve the host's pressing social responsibility?

_____

_____

_____

_____

b. Jesus' response to His mother (John 2:4) may seem abrasive. Although the original Greek meaning of the word **woman** is much less abrupt than our modern use of the word, Jesus was still making a point. What was Jesus conveying by addressing his mother as **woman** rather than "mother" (John 2:4; Luke 2:41–49)?

Use a pen to record your answers. You will be able to read them in the future if you lead another person or group through this same study.

ADDITIONAL INSIGHTS

_____

_____

_____

3. Many people are confused about Mary's true identity. Some venerate her as a god-like figure and co-redempter with Jesus, while others relegate her to the position of an insignificant pawn used by God. What does the Bible teach about this amazing woman (Luke 1:26–28, 38, 46–47; John 19:25–27)?

_____

_____

_____

_____

_____

_____

_____

4. Jesus addressed his mother as **woman** and told her **My hour has not yet come** (John 2:4). Mary appears to have been unfazed, however, instructing the servants to do whatever Jesus said (John 2:5). Why do you think Jesus met the need for more wine when it appeared He had not planned to do so originally?

_____

_____

_____

5. It was the custom of Jews to use water for purification in the event they touched a Gentile or anything else that might defile them. As such, the host arranged to have at

the wedding a generous supply of water for purification purposes (six jars holding a total of approximately 120–180 gallons), but he miscalculated the amount of wine the guests would consume.

a. What specific things did Jesus instruct the servants to do to alleviate this serious problem (John 2:6–10)?

_____

_____

_____

_____

b. John 2:6–10 does not say that Jesus actually turned water into wine; it states that the water in the **waterpots** (NIV: "water jars") became wine when it was poured out (John 2:9). How do we know for sure that Jesus actually turned the water into wine (John 2:11; 4:46)?

_____

_____

_____

6. Some Christians use the example of Jesus turning water into wine as biblical support for drinking alcohol. What does the Bible teach regarding the believer's use of wine (sometimes symbolic for "intoxicating beverages") and other alcoholic beverages for non-medicinal purposes (Proverbs 20:1; 23:29–35; 31:4–7; Romans 14:21)?

_____

_____

_____

_____

_____

_____

7. The New Testament records thirty-five miracles performed by Jesus. The apostle John uses the word **signs** (Gk. *semeion*) to point people to the significance of miracles rather than the events themselves. What were two results of Jesus' turning water into wine (John 2:11).

_____

_____

8. Jesus and His mother, His brothers (see Matthew 13:55 for his brothers' names), and a number of new disciples went down (east; biblical directional designations are based on elevation) to Capernaum for a brief time. Later, Jesus and His disciples went up (south) to Jerusalem to attend the Passover Feast. All Jewish men twenty years and older were required to attend the three annual pilgrim feasts in Jerusalem, including Passover.

   a. Jews traveling to Jerusalem for the Passover normally would exchange their Tyrian coinage for Greek or Roman money so they could pay the temple tax and buy animals to sacrifice. What happened when Jesus saw the temple turned into a stockyard overrun with greedy merchants (John 2:14–16)?

_____

_____

_____

_____

   b. How did the Jews respond to Jesus' rebuke of their evil practices (John 2:18)?

_____

_____

_____

_____

9. While Jesus was in Jerusalem for the Passover, He performed signs (John 2:23), and as a result, many believed in His name. However, Jesus did not commit Himself to them (John 2:24). What do you think that meant?

_____

_____

_____

_____

_____

FOUR

YOU MUST BE BORN AGAIN

Read John 3; other references as given.

Jesus cleansing the temple must have been quite a scene— sheep and oxen turning over tables as both money changers and animals alike were driven out of the outer court ... gold and silver coins noisily spilling onto the limestone floor ... people yelling ... confusion everywhere (see John 2:13–21). By nightfall, all of Jerusalem certainly was abuzz about the young rabbi's actions, including a Pharisee named Nicodemus (nick-oh-DEE-mus).

This lesson focuses on two discourses: one in Jerusalem between Nicodemus and Jesus (John 3:1–21), and the other in Judea between John the Baptist and his disciples (John 3:22–36). Both scenarios provide life-changing spiritual truths for those willing to receive them.

Before you begin, please ask God to reveal Himself through His Word and to give you grace to accept the truths you will be learning.

1. Nicodemus was a member of the Pharisee religious sect (John 3:1). Pharisees (from the Greek verb *phares,* to separate) were a strict religious party numbering about 6,000 during Jesus' life on earth. The Pharisees' origin is somewhat obscure, but their doctrine was clear: strict adherence to the Law of Moses and the oral teachings of Jewish rabbis. They adopted innumerable manmade regulations that externalized their religious experience, deadened their sensitivity toward God, and made them hypercritical toward others.

59:59 Rule:

Participants appreciate when the leader starts and finishes the studies on time—all in one hour (the 59:59 rule). If the leader doesn't complete the entire lesson, the participants will be less likely to do their weekly lessons and the Bible study discussion will tend to wander.

ADD GROUP INSIGHTS BELOW

a.   Who did Nicodemus understand Jesus to be (John 3:2)?

_____

_____

b.   Although Nicodemus did not voice his concern,
     Jesus answered his implied question ("Who really are
     you?") with a foundational statement. What did Jesus
     tell Nicodemus must happen to him before he could
     understand who He is or begin to comprehend the
     kingdom of God (John 3:3)?

_____

_____

2.   The phrase **a ruler of the Jews** (John 3:1) indicates that
     Nicodemus also was a member of the Sanhedrin, an
     administrative body of seventy (or seventy-two) Jewish
     leaders who attempted to govern the religious and daily
     lives of the Jewish people. As a member of the Sanhedrin,
     Nicodemus likely would have been a scribe, well-versed in
     the Old Testament Law.

     a.   How did Nicodemus understand Jesus' statement,
          **unless one is born again, he cannot see the king-
          dom of God** (John 3:4)?

_____

_____

     b.   What was Jesus' answer to Nicodemus (John 3:5–8)?

_____

_____

_____

     c.   Jesus said **You must be born again** (John 3:7). He
          didn't suggest it would be a good idea to be born
          again. Are you *absolutely* certain you have been

born again according to the Bible? _____ If so, when and where did your spiritual conversion occur? _____ If you are not certain, is there anything preventing you from trusting Jesus Christ as your Lord and Savior right now?

_____

_____

_____

ADDITIONAL INSIGHTS

3.   The phrase **born of water and the Spirit** is difficult to interpret (John 3:5). At least five interpretations have been offered: (1) the water refers to the natural birth and the Spirit to the new birth; (2) the water refers to the Word of God (Ephesians 5:26); (3) the water refers to baptism as a necessary part of regeneration; (4) the water is a symbol of the Holy Spirit (John 7:37–39; cf. Ezekiel 36:24–27)—a concept Nicodemus easily would have understood; and (5) the water refers to John the Baptist's ministry of repentance, and the Spirit refers to the Holy Spirit's work of regeneration. Which view do you think is the best interpretation of this difficult phrase? Why?

_____

_____

_____

_____

_____

_____

4.   As is the case with many religious people today, Nicodemus's salvation-by-works background hindered his ability to understand salvation by grace (John 3:9). What two things does Jesus say in response to Nicodemus's question about the new birth (John 3:10)?

_____

_____

_____

_____

_____

5. In John 3:14 Jesus used a powerful Old Testament illustration to help Nicodemus understand the new birth. During the Exodus, God sent fiery serpents among the Israelites to punish them for their grumbling against God and Moses (Numbers 21:5–6). God instructed Moses to make a bronze serpent and place it on a pole as an object lesson and as a remedy for the deadly plague. Those who looked at the bronze pole were healed, and their lives were saved (Numbers 21:8–9).

   a. Name at least four similarities between the "fiery serpent" illustration and the new birth (Numbers 21:5–9; John 3:14–16).

_____

_____

_____

_____

   b. All those who looked at the fiery brass serpent were healed physically, and their lives were spared (Numbers 21:8). Who today is able to be healed spiritually (born again or saved) (John 3:15–16)?

_____

_____

_____

On what basis do people receive eternal life?

_____

_____

_____

c. What happens to those who do not believe (trust) in Jesus Christ (John 3:15, 18)?

_____

_____

_____

d. The consequences of someone not trusting in Jesus Christ's substitutionary sacrifice for salvation are horrifying. Why is it that anyone doesn't come to Christ and accept His offer of salvation (John 3:19–20)?

_____

_____

_____

e. Knowing the eternal consequences for those who die without trusting Christ, what should all Christians be doing (John 4:35; 1 Corinthians 9:19–22; 2 Corinthians 5:11, 20)?

_____

_____

_____

_____

6. Jesus traveled south into the countryside of Judea where He oversaw His disciples as they baptized new converts (John 3:22; 4:2). At the same time John the Baptist also was baptizing new converts in Aenon (John 3:23, likely located on the west side of the Jordan River midway between the Sea of Galilee and the Dead Sea [Samaria]) when a controversy developed with Jewish leaders over purification (John 3:25). In addition, John's disciples were troubled that Jesus was gaining more followers than they were (John 3:26). John used their concerns to point his followers to Christ and away from himself.

a. In John 3:27–31, John the Baptist provided five convincing reasons (one in each verse) why his followers should embrace Christ and regard Him as superior. What are they?

_____

_____

_____

_____

_____

_____

_____

_____

_____

_____

b. John the Baptist said **God does not give the Spirit by measure** (John 3:34, NIV: "God gives the Spirit without limit"). What do you think that means?

_____

_____

_____

_____

7. John 3:36 serves as a sobering warning to those who reject Christ and a powerful motivator to believers. What is the present condition of the unsaved, and what will happen to them if they never are saved?

_____

_____

FIVE

TOTAL
REFRESHMENT

Read John 4;
other references as given.

The Bible often uses contrasting characters to teach powerful spiritual truths. From the story of David and Goliath (1 Samuel 17), we learn that unwavering faith in God overcomes overwhelming obstacles. From the story of the Good Samaritan (Luke 10:30–36), we learn that genuine compassion often comes from unexpected sources (the Samaritan) and that God's people (Levites, priests) often can be unmerciful and unloving.

Another powerful contrast of characters appears in John, chapters 3 and 4. In John 3 we met Nicodemus—Jewish, male, respectable, educated, moral, a teacher of the law, but spiritually lost. In John 4 we meet an unnamed woman—half-Jewish, disrespectable, uneducated, immoral, but spiritually redeemed by Christ.

Before you begin, please ask God to reveal Himself through His Word and to give you grace to accept the truths you will be learning.

Focus Rule:

If the leader helps the group members focus on the Bible, they will gain more confidence to study God's Word on their own.

ADD GROUP
INSIGHTS BELOW

1. Jesus left Judea and traveled north to Galilee (John 4:1–3; Galilee was [and still is] the region west and north of the Sea of Galilee). There were three standard travel routes from Jerusalem to Galilee—a westerly one along the coastal plain, an easterly one along the Jordan River, and a third, less desirable one that went directly north along the Judean mountain ridge. The last route passed directly through Samaria, where ethnic hostility occasionally erupted into

open conflict, resulting in death for unwary travelers.

a. The statement **He needed to go through Samaria** (John 4:4) and Jesus' subsequent encounter with an immoral woman at a well (John 4:7–30) indicates He intentionally went through Samaria to reach her and other Samaritans with the message of eternal life. List at least two additional things this teaches about Jesus' desire to reach the lost.

_____

_____

_____

b. If you are a Christian, what specific things are you doing to reach others with the message of salvation?

_____

_____

_____

2. The Samaritans were a mixed race of Jewish and Gentile origin that practiced a syncretistic form of worship consisting of mixed Judaistic and pagan beliefs. A small group of Samaritans today still practices their ancient religion. List two reasons why the Samaritan woman was surprised that Jesus asked her for a drink (John 4:7–9).

_____

_____

3. Jesus stopped about noon to rest at Jacob's Well (John 4:6). Archeologists today believe an ancient well located 1½ miles southwest of the Samaritan city of Sychar is Jacob's Well (currently known as Jacob's Spring). The water in Jacob's Spring is particularly refreshing, leading many to believe a spring feeds the well at the bottom.

a. Jesus' interaction with the Samaritan woman is a model example of personal evangelism—one that can teach believers a great deal. Look closely at Jesus' approach and the Samaritan woman's reactions. How did Jesus' response to the woman's first question increase her curiosity (John 4:10–12)?

_____

_____

_____

_____

_____

_____

b. Write two interesting questions you could use as an opener in a witnessing conversation with another person—questions possessing both a connection to his or her present circumstances and an element of spiritual intrigue.

_____

_____

_____

4. The Samaritan woman was intrigued by Jesus' offer to provide **living** (Gk. *pege*: well, spring) **water**, even though she was thinking in natural terms. It is likely the woman wanted to know how Jesus could get to the spring water at the bottom of the well, especially since He didn't even have a bucket (John 4:11).

a. How did Jesus gracefully move the conversation from physical water to the woman's need for living water (John 4:13–14)?

_____

_____

If the leader places a watch on the table, participants will feel confident that the Bible study will be completed on time. If the leader doesn't complete the lesson each week, participants will be less likely to do their weekly lessons, and the discussion will not be as rich.

ADDITIONAL INSIGHTS

_____

_____

b. What is the **living water** (John 4:10, 14)?

_____

_____

5. In John 4:16, Jesus appears to interrupt His conversation about living water by asking the woman to invite her husband to join them.

a. Jesus' request to have the woman's husband join them reveals an important truth about personal witnessing that often is missing from many modern gospel presentations (John 4:16–19). What is it?

_____

_____

_____

_____

_____

b. What did Jesus say to the Samaritan woman when she attempted to sidetrack the conversation onto the worship differences between Jews and Samaritans (John 4:21–24)?

_____

_____

_____

6. What do you think it means to worship God **in spirit and truth** (John 4:23–24)?

_____

_____

7. The woman left her waterpot and went into the city to invite others to meet Jesus (John 4:28–29). Her statement **Come, see a Man who told me all things that I ever did. Could this be the Christ?** (John 4:29) has been variously interpreted as (1) an overzealous (and incorrect) statement of a new believer, (2) a correct summary of the important event(s) of her life, or (3) an intriguing statement in the form of a question designed to spawn curiosity among the men (perhaps some with whom she had been intimate).

   a. What important truths did Jesus teach His disciples about the spiritual harvest (John 4:35)?

   _____

   _____

   _____

   b. I low did the men of Sychar respond to the woman's appeal and their time with Jesus (4:39–42)?

   _____

8. Many Christians are afraid to share their faith in Christ. Some experience ongoing guilt, believing they've failed the Lord and any unsaved person who doesn't respond immediately in faith. What important spiritual truths are taught in the following verses about personal evangelism: John 4:36–38; Matthew 9:37–38; Mark 1:17?

   _____

   _____

   _____

   _____

   _____

   _____

41

9. Jesus stayed with the Samaritans for two days before he continued north to Cana of Galilee, where He had turned water into wine (John 4:45–46). Likely, the Galileans received Him gladly because they remembered His bold attack on the moneychangers and were grateful He'd corrected such an injustice.

    a. In John 20:30–31, this gospel points out that Jesus had performed many other signs, but **these are written that you may believe that Jesus is the Christ, the Son of God**. In what ways was the healing of the nobleman's son (the second sign) different from the first sign of Jesus turning water into wine (John 2:7–11; 4:46–53)?

        _____

        _____

    b. How should Jesus' power and willingness to heal the nobleman's son from a distance affect a believer's confidence in prayer?

        _____

        _____

        _____

Six

Is Jesus Equal With God?

**Read John 5;
other references as given.**

In John 4, Jesus traveled north through Samaria into Galilee where He performed the second sign (healing of the nobleman's son, John 4:46–54). The signs manifested Christ's glory (revealed His divine nature) so that those who observed them might believe that Jesus is the Christ. The first sign revealed Jesus' power over nature, and the second sign revealed His power over disease.

During Jesus' first visit to Jerusalem (John 2:13–21), He overturned the greedy moneychangers' tables and drove them and their animals from the temple. In John 5, Jesus returns to Jerusalem, where He performs a miracle on the Sabbath that gives the Jewish leaders—already angry from His previous actions—more reason to persecute Him.

Before you begin, please ask God to reveal Himself through His Word and to give you grace to accept the truths you will be learning.

1. The phrase **After this** (John 5:1; NIV: "some time later") refers to an unspecified period of time before Jesus returned to Jerusalem to attend another Jewish feast. In Jerusalem, Jesus visited the Pool of Bethesda that had five porches, or covered colonnades, under which many sick people lay. In 1888, workers making repairs on the Church of St. Anne found the Pool of Bethesda.

Drawing Rule:

To learn how to include everyone in the group discussion over a period of time, go to www. Lamplighters USA.org/training or call 800 507-9516.

ADD GROUP INSIGHTS BELOW

43

a. The water possessed a therapeutic benefit when it was stirred (perhaps similar to a hot spring) and the infirmed entered the pool in the hopes of being healed (John 5:3–7). What question did Jesus ask the man who had been paralyzed for thirty-eight years?

_____

_____

b. How did Jesus know the man still desired to be healed after thirty-eight years of physical disability (John 5:7)?

_____

_____

2. The earliest Greek manuscripts (the basis for all New Testament translations) do not include the last phrase in verse three (**waiting for the moving of the water**) and all of verse four. Some English translations (KJV, NKJV, NASB) include them, but others (NIV, ESV) include them only as a footnote or side reference. Christians may be tempted to doubt the inspiration of the Bible when they encounter a manuscript variance such as this. Why do you think, in such situations, a believer's confidence in the Bible as the inspired Word of God should not be disputed?

_____

_____

_____

_____

_____

3. Jesus asked the invalid of thirty-eight years, **Do you want to be made well?** (John 5:6). Similar to Jesus' previous question to John's disciples, **What do you seek?** (John 1:38), this question also could be construed in various ways: "Do you want to be *physically* healed?" "Do you want to be made *spiritually* whole?" "Do you really want to be

made well, or do you prefer to have your material needs met through begging?"

a. What attitude does God want Christians to have toward those who are sick or physically disabled (Luke 10:30–37; John 9:1–3; 1 Corinthians 11:27–30; James 5:14–16)?

_____

_____

_____

_____

b. How did the apostle Paul view the afflictions God allowed into his life, including health-related afflictions (2 Corinthians 12:9–10)?

_____

_____

4. On the Sabbath Jesus healed the man who had been disabled for thirty-eight years (the third sign). The rabbis taught that thirty-nine principal works were forbidden to be done on the Sabbath, including performing the household chore of carrying a mat (which Jesus had instructed the invalid to do). What was the reaction of the Jewish leaders to the miraculous healing of the man on the Sabbath (John 5:8–16)?

_____

_____

_____

5. As you study the Gospels, it is important to realize that Jesus did three things as He ministered: (1) He manifested His glory so that people might come to believe that He is the Christ, (2) He attempted to draw people back to the Word of God and away from their man-made religious traditions, and

(3) He trained His disciples to reach the world after His death (Matthew 28:18–20).

a. Jesus healed a man who had been disabled for thirty-eight years, but the Jewish leaders were more concerned about the fact that the man carried his mat on the Sabbath. Name at least four spiritual problems that occur when we allow man-made traditions to become part of our religious experience (Mark 7:1–9).

_____

_____

_____

_____

_____

b. Many Christians are quick to identify man-made (nonbiblical) religious traditions held by other believers, but they aren't so adept at seeing them in their own lives. What man-made religious traditions do you believe to be true that actually have no scriptural basis—beliefs that may be causing you to disobey God's Word?

_____

_____

_____

_____

6. When Jesus answered the Jewish authorities' accusations about healing the paralytic on the Sabbath, He taught several important truths about His divine nature. Identify a truth from each of the following verse divisions: John 5:17–18; 19, 20, 21, 22–30; Psalm 121:3–4.

_____

_____

_____

_____

_____

_____

7. In John 5:17–30, Jesus made four bold statements about His true nature. After excluding Himself as a witness of His own works (they were from God; John 5:31), Jesus called four witnesses to testify to His divinity (John 5:32-39).

   a. Who were the four witnesses (John 5:32–35; 36; 37–38; 39)?

   _____

   _____

   _____

   _____

   b. What mistake did the Jews make in their study of the Scriptures that often is repeated by many Christians today (John 5:39)?

   _____

   _____

   _____

   c. What is the difference, if any, between being a diligent student of the Bible and having a dynamic relationship with Jesus Christ?

   _____

   _____

8. Why were the Jews not able to receive His teachings (John 5:40–44)?

   _____

   _____

9. a. What do you think is the meaning of the phrase **there
        is one who accuses you—Moses, in whom you trust**
        (John 5:45)?

    _____

    _____

    _____

    _____

    b. Jesus said that Moses wrote about Him (John 5:46),
        meaning that the Pentateuch (the first five books of the
        Bible) is more than the story of creation and God dealing
        with infant Israel—the Pentateuch contains glimpses of
        the person of Jesus Christ and references to His work.
        What did Jesus tell the two travelers on the road to
        Emmaus that confirmed this truth (Luke 24:27)?

    _____

    _____

    _____

    _____

    _____

SEVEN

I AM THE BREAD OF LIFE

> ## Read John 6;
> ## other references as given.

In John 5, the Jewish religious leaders were so enraged that Jesus healed the paralytic on the Sabbath that they planned to kill him (John 5:16). Jesus' subsequent declaration that He is equal with God likely increased their hatred and strengthened their resolve to destroy Him.

In John 6, Jesus traveled north to Galilee where He performed the miracle of feeding the five thousand. Of Jesus' thirty-five recorded miracles, this is the only one mentioned in all four gospels. The miracle was followed by one of Jesus' most powerful sermons—*I Am the Bread of Life* sermon (John 6:35–58). The Jewish religious leaders rejected His claim as the true bread of heaven, and even many of His disciples abandoned Him.

Before you begin, please ask God to reveal Himself through His Word and to give you grace to accept the truths you will be learning.

Gospel Gold Rule:

Try to get all the answers to the questions—not just the easy ones. Go for the gold.

ADD GROUP INSIGHTS BELOW

1. During the final year of Jesus' ministry, multitudes of people followed Him wherever He went (John 6:2). Some followed because they wanted Him to be their ruler (John 6:15), others followed for the things He provided (John 6:26), and still others wanted to see the signs He performed (John 6:30). With His death less than a year away, Jesus needed to sift the wheat from the tares (the true believers from the shallow, fleshly followers) and prepare true disciples for His coming crucifixion.

a. The feeding of the five thousand (the fourth sign) occurred on the northeast corner of the Sea of Galilee near the city of Bethsaida (Luke 9:10). Bible commentators estimate there were ten to twenty thousand people present at the time. Why do you think Jesus tested Philip by asking where they could buy bread when He knew what He was going to do (John 6:5–6)?

_____

_____

_____

b. Think of a time when God tested you. What did you learn about God and yourself in the process? Be prepared to share your answers with others.

_____

_____

_____

2. Jesus performed a miracle by feeding between five and twenty thousand people from five barley loaves (Gk. *artos*: round, pancake-like flatbread) and two small fish. Many people attempt to deny the supernatural by defining miracles from a human perspective. Christian Scientists, for example, define *miracle* as "a divinely natural phenomenon experienced humanly as a fulfillment of spiritual law."

a. What is a miracle? Use a dictionary to help you, if you'd like.

_____

_____

b. What was the response of those who witnessed the miraculous feeding of the five thousand (John 6:14–15)?

_____

_____

c.   What was Jesus' response to those who wanted to take Him by force and make Him king (John 6:15)?

_____

_____

3.   Jesus sent the disciples across the Sea of Galilee to Capernaum while He prayed alone on the mountainside. When a fierce storm arose on the lake and the disciples were in great peril, Jesus walked on the water beside them (the fifth sign) and calmed the storm (John 6:19; Mark 6:48–52). The disciples were amazed at Jesus' power to calm the storm, and they worshipped Him. What had the disciples learned from the feeding-of-the-five-thousand miracle earlier that same day (Mark 6:51–52)?

_____

_____

_____

4.   The next day, people who had witnessed the miraculous feeding of the five thousand realized that Jesus was gone, so they went to Capernaum to find Him (John 6:22–25).

a.   What did Jesus say to the people about their motivation to follow Him (John 6:26)?

_____

_____

b.   The people asked a profound question that every person should consider asking: **What shall we do, that we may work the works of God?** (John 6:28; NLT: "What does God want us to do?") What answer did Jesus give (John 6:29)?

_____

_____

Would you like to learn how to lead someone through this same study? It's not hard. Go to www.Lamplighters USA.org to register for *free* online leadership training.

ADDITIONAL INSIGHTS

51

c. What did the people say that indicated they completely misunderstood Jesus' answer (John 6:30–31)?

_____

_____

_____

5. The people weren't convinced they should place their complete faith in Jesus. After all, they believed in Moses and followed Mosaic law, and Moses had called down bread from *heaven* (John 6:31). Jesus had only multiplied *earthly* bread to feed five thousand. Because, to them, Moses' miraculous provision was superior, they were hesitant to place their trust in Jesus. Name four things Jesus told the people about the bread from heaven to help them understand who He was (John 6:32–33).

_____

_____

_____

_____

_____

_____

6. Jesus' bread-of-life sermon is an excellent explanation of how a person comes to saving faith in Jesus Christ. List at least five truths about how we are brought to salvation (John 6:35–40).

_____

_____

_____

_____

_____

_____

_____

_____

Has your group
become a "Holy
huddle?" Learn
how to reach out
to others by taking
online leadership
training.

ADDITIONAL
INSIGHTS

7. The Jewish leaders took offense at Jesus' statement **I am the bread which came down from heaven** (John 6:41) and murmured among themselves (John 6:43).

   a. What did Jesus tell the Jewish leaders was the reason why they couldn't understand or comprehend His true identity (John 6:44–45)?

   _____

   _____

   _____

   b. What must a person do in order to receive the gift of eternal life (John 6:47)?

   _____

   _____

8. Throughout John's gospel there is a repeated call to believe (John 3:16, 18, 36; 5:24; 6:40). Those who don't believe are condemned (John 3:36), and yet John 6:44 says that no one can come to Christ unless God draws them. How do you think people can be commanded to believe (and be held accountable for their unbelief) if they cannot come to Christ until God draws them?

   _____

   _____

   _____

   _____

9. a. Jesus answered the Jews' question **How can this Man give us His flesh to eat?** (John 6:52) with a vivid illustration of the "exchanged-life" principle. What do

you think Jesus meant when he said **unless you eat the flesh of the Son of Man and drink His blood, you have no life in you** (John 6:53)?

_____

_____

_____

   b. How did some of Jesus' disciples react when they heard Him speak about eating His flesh and drinking His blood (John 6:60–61, 66)?

_____

_____

_____

10. Having just "sifted the wheat from the tares," Jesus turned to the twelve apostles and asked if they also wanted to leave (John 6:67). Peter's answer is a quintessential or typical statement of every true disciple of Jesus Christ: **Lord, to whom shall we go? You have the words of eternal life** (John 6:68). If you were one of Jesus' original followers and you knew the days of adoring crowds had passed and times of intense persecution lay ahead, how do you think you would have answered Jesus' question, **"Do you also want to go away?"** (John 6:67)?

_____

_____

_____

_____

_____

_____

EIGHT

LIFE'S MOST IMPORTANT QUESTION

Read John 7; other references as given.

Who is Jesus? This is the most important question you'll ever be asked. And everyone must answer this question, including you. The question cannot be ignored, avoided, dismissed, or trivialized. You *must* answer the question, and no one can answer it for you.

In John 7, we find several groups of people struggling to understand who Jesus is. How could Jesus be so wise if He didn't study in the best rabbinic schools? Could Jesus possibly be demon-possessed? If Jesus is from Galilee, He couldn't be the Messiah, could He? In this lesson you'll see people wrestling with the question, "Who is Jesus?" in the same way people do today.

Before you begin, please ask God to reveal Himself through His Word and to give you grace to accept the truths you will be learning.

1. The phrase **After these things** (John 7:1) refers to the intervening months between Passover in early spring (John 6:4) and the Feast of Tabernacles that began on the fifteenth day of the seventh month (John 7:2, roughly the second week of October). During this time, Jesus ministered throughout northern Galilee (Matthew 14:34–18:14). Why did Jesus' younger brothers (James, Joses, Simon, and Judas; Matthew 13:55) strongly urge Him to attend the Feast of Tabernacles in Jerusalem (John 7:3–4)?

Balance Rule:

To learn how to balance the group discussion, go to www.Lamplighters USA.org/training or call 800 507-9516.

ADD GROUP INSIGHTS BELOW

_____

_____

_____

_____

2. Many Christians struggle to understand God's will for their lives even though the Bible teaches, **Therefore do not be unwise, but understand what the will of the Lord is** (Ephesians 5:17). Jesus' response to His brothers— somewhat reminiscent of the one He gave His mother (John 2:4)—teaches an important principle about understanding and then doing God's will.

    a. How can a believer consistently discern God's will for his life (Judges 18:5–6; Proverbs 3:5; 11:14; Romans 12:1–2)?

    _____

    _____

    _____

    _____

    b. What important principle about following God's will is emphasized in Jesus' response to His brothers (John 7:6, 8)?

    _____

    _____

3. Jesus' brothers went to the feast, but He stayed behind in Galilee. Sometime later Jesus (and probably His disciples) went **in secret** (John 7:10). Likely Jesus traveled covertly in late evening along secondary roads to avoid recognition. What were the people saying about Jesus in Jerusalem (John 7:11–12, 15, 20)?

    _____

_____

_____

_____

Having trouble with your group? A Lamplighters trainer can help you solve the problem.

_____

ADDITIONAL INSIGHTS

4. Some people attempt to discover Jesus' true identity by using a purely academic approach. They believe their reasoning is unbiased and objective, but they fail to understand their own spiritual condition and their inability to understand God without divine intervention.

    a. Why can't the natural (unsaved, not born again) person comprehend Jesus' true identity without divine assistance (John 3:19–20; 1 Corinthians 2:14; 2 Corinthians 4:4)?

    _____

    _____

    _____

    b. What did John the Baptist say about receiving spiritual truth (John 3:27)?

    _____

    _____

    c. What must a person do in order to understand correct-doctrine or spiritual truth (John 7:17)?

    _____

    _____

5. The Jews boasted that they were Moses' disciples (John 9:28), but they didn't obey his teaching. Jesus exposed their hypocrisy by reminding them, "If you are truly followers of Moses, you wouldn't be trying to kill Me, because it is a violation of the sixth commandment, 'You shall not murder'" (John 7:19, author paraphrase). Jesus then used a second argument—the rite of circumcision performed on the eighth

day—to reveal their faulty reasoning. Explain the argument Jesus used to expose the inconsistency of the Jews' thinking (John 7:19–23, the **one work** [NIV: "one miracle," v. 21]) regarding His healing of the paralytic on the Sabbath.

_____

_____

_____

_____

_____

6. The Feast of Tabernacles (Leviticus 23:33–43; Numbers 29:12–39, also called the Feast of Booths) was the Jews' annual harvest festival. It was a joyous week of celebration that followed immediately after the Day of Atonement, when the national sins of the Jewish people were forgiven. During the Feast, families lived in temporary shelters or leafy booths constructed to commemorate their wilderness wanderings during the Exodus. The temple trumpets were blown each day, and water from the Pool of Siloam was poured out in remembrance of God's miraculous provisions of water at Meribah (Exodus 17:1–7) and rains for their crops. The temple's inner court was lit with large candlesticks to commemorate the pillar of fire God had provided to guide the Israelites during the exodus.

    a. As Jesus taught boldly in the temple, people murmured among themselves about Jesus' true identity and wondered why the religious leaders were not doing anything to stop Him (John 7:26). What were the various reactions of the people during that time (John 7:26–32, 40–49)?

        _____

        _____

        _____

        _____

b. Where have you observed similar reactions to the person of Jesus Christ?

_____

_____

_____

It's a good time to begin praying and inviting new people for your next Open House.

c. What did Jesus mean when He said, **You will seek Me and not find Me, and where I am you cannot come** (John 7:34)?

_____

_____

_____

ADDITIONAL
INSIGHTS

7. Jesus used a previous illustration—**living water** (Gk. *pege*, well, spring, living)—to compare the water being poured out at the Feast of Tabernacles to the true spiritual refreshment He could provide everyone (John 7:37–38).

a. What two prerequisites are necessary to receive the **living water** Jesus offers (John 7:37–38)?

_____

_____

_____

b. Look back at lesson number 5, *Living Water*, question 4(b). What, if anything, could you now add to your answer to make it more complete?

_____

_____

8. The religious leaders sent officers to arrest Jesus (John 7:32), but they returned empty-handed, much to the dismay of the Jewish leaders (John 7:45–46).

a. What two negative attitudes did the Jewish leaders display during their brief interaction with the officers that prevented them from understanding the truth (John 7:47–49)?

_____

_____

b. How does Nicodemus's attitude differ from other members of the Sanhedrin (John 7:50–52)?

_____

_____

_____

c. Many Jews couldn't receive spiritual truth because of their pride. Is there something in your life that prevents you from receiving spiritual truth (pride, a secret sin, fear of people, denominational pressure, family loyalty, etc.)?

_____

_____

_____

_____

NINE

I AM THE LIGHT OF THE WORLD

Jesus was the focal point of intense debate in John 7. Some said Jesus was good (John 7:12), some said He was a deceiver (John 7:12), and others thought He was demon-possessed (John 7:20). But there were others who believed in Him and said He was the Christ (John 7:31, 41). Many people legitimately were confused (John 7:27, 41), but others — blinded by their own spiritual pride — hardened their hearts and refused to believe. Certainly, the apostle John's earlier words were being fulfilled: **He [Jesus] came to His own, and His own did not receive Him** (John 1:11).

After Jesus fed the five thousand, He presented Himself as the true **bread of life** (John 6). In John 8, Jesus follows the same pattern and uses the imagery of the torchlights at the Feast of Tabernacles and presents Himself as the true **light of the world** (John 8:12). Jesus reminds His listeners that only He can redeem people and enable them to overcome spiritual darkness (blindness to the reality of God and the consequences of their own sin).

Before you begin, please ask God to reveal Himself through His Word and to give you grace to accept the truths you will be learning.

1. The day after Jesus presented Himself as the true bread of life, He went to the temple where He sat down and taught (John 8:2). The scribes and the Pharisees brought

No-Trespassing Rule:

To keep the Bible study on track, avoid talking about political parties, church denominations, and Bible translations.

ADD GROUP INSIGHTS BELOW

a woman caught in the act of adultery, intending to trap Jesus (John 8:6). If He condemned the immoral woman, His popular support as a "friend of sinners" would dissipate quickly, and the religious leaders could take Him by force. If Jesus refused to condemn her, He would be violating the law of Moses. Either answer would accomplish the wicked goals of the religious leaders. If you were in Jesus' place and powerful religious leaders were pressing you for an immediate response, what would you have said or done?

_____

_____

_____

_____

2. Jesus' response to the scribes and Pharisees is absolutely profound. Jesus' words reveal three important principles Christians can use when they counsel other believers. Now look carefully at His initial response to the religious leaders (John 8:7).

a. Jesus said to the woman's accusers **He who is without sin among you, let him throw a stone at her first** (John 8:7). Now restate Jesus' words to the accusers in the form of a principle by completing the following sentence: *When counseling someone caught in sin, the first thing to do is* ....

_____

_____

_____

b. Jesus' words **Has no one condemned you? Neither do I condemn you** (John 8:10–11) reveal the second principle. Now state this principle in your own words.

_____

_____

3. At first glance Jesus' words **Go and sin no more** (John 8:11) seem simplistic and inadequate. After all, doesn't she need sexual addiction therapy, months or years of counseling, and a weekly support group?

   a. What is the third important principle that is embedded in Jesus' final words to the woman **go and sin no more** (John 8:11; 1 Corinthians 10:13)?

   _____

   _____

   _____

   b. If you are a Christian, are you excusing a sin (lust, anger, pride, hatred, covetousness, malice, sexual impurity, illicit drug use, etc.) that you know is wrong? Are you justifying your sin rather than trusting God to overcome it and the temptations you are facing?

   _____

   _____

   _____

4. After the incident with the religious leaders and the adulterous woman, Jesus continued to teach the people, saying He is the light of the world. Those who follow Him will not **walk in darkness, but have the light of life** (John 8:12). What does that mean?

   _____

   _____

   _____

   _____

   _____

   _____

Want to learn how to disciple another person, lead a life-changing Bible study or start another study? Go to www.Lamplighters USA.org/training to learn how.

ADDITIONAL INSIGHTS

5. How did the religious leaders respond to such a profound truth (John 8:13)?

_____

6. Jesus stated several things that are true about the spiritual condition, both now and after death, of those who are not saved. List at least four (John 8:21–24).

_____

_____

_____

_____

_____

_____

7. Jesus continued to preach to the people in the face of intense hostility and unjustified scrutiny. In spite of the resistance, many believed (John 8:30).

   a. What did Jesus tell those who believed in Him (John 8:31–32)?

   _____

   _____

   b. What do you think it means to **abide in** (Gk. *meno*—to remain, NIV: "hold to") Jesus' Word (John 8:31)?

   _____

   _____

   _____

   c. **If you abide in My Word, you are My [Jesus'] disciples indeed** (John 8:31, NIV: "really my disciples"). The corollary is that those who do not abide in His Word aren't really His true or convicted disciples. Based on the definition of the Greek word *meno* (to remain), do you qualify to be one of Jesus' true or convicted disciples? What changes would you have to make in your life to qualify to be one of Jesus' true disciples?

_____

_____

_____

8. a. What did Jesus say about those who practice sin (John 8:34–35)?

_____

_____

_____

   b. What did the apostle Paul say about the believer's relationship with habitual sin (Romans 6:17–22)?

_____

_____

_____

9. Once again, the Jewish authorities attacked Jesus' character. This time they attacked His earthly heritage, implying that His birth was illegitimate (John 8:41). His mysterious birth and the presence of a Roman garrison not far from Nazareth led the Jews to imply Jesus' birth was illegitimate. How did Jesus respond to the accusation (John 8:42–45)?

_____

_____

_____

10. The Jewish leaders increased their attack, saying **You are a Samaritan and have a demon** (John 8:48). Considering the fact that the Jews hated the Samaritans, they couldn't

have said anything worse about Him. Jesus denied their accusation and continued to preach, saying that **if anyone keeps My Word he shall never see death** (John 8:51).

a. What did Jesus mean when he said **he shall never see death** (John 8:51)?

_____

_____

b. How did the Jews misunderstand Jesus' teaching on this subject (John 8:52–53, 57)?

_____

_____

11. a. What did Jesus say that made the Jews want to stone Him (John 8:58)?

_____

_____

b. What was Jesus saying about Himself when He spoke those words?

_____

_____

_____

TEN

THE MESSIANIC MIRACLE

Read John 9;
other references as given.

Thirty-five of Jesus' miracles are recorded in the Gospels. Twenty-three involve healing the sick or disabled, nine demonstrate His power over nature, and three manifest His power over death. Jesus healed men and women, adults and children, Jews and Gentiles, believers and nonbelievers.

In John 8, Jesus borrowed a powerful image from the torchlights at the Feast of Tabernacles and identified Himself as the light of the world (John 8:12). In John 9, Jesus authenticated His claim to be the light of the world by giving a blind man sight and fulfilling several Old Testament prophecies (Isaiah 29:18, 35:5, 42:7) to prove He was the Messiah.

Before you begin, please ask God to reveal Himself through His Word and to give you grace to accept the truths you will be learning.

Transformation Rule:

Seek for personal transformation, not mere information, from God's Word.

ADD GROUP INSIGHTS BELOW

1. What was the disciples' initial reaction when they saw the blind man (John 9:2)?

_____

_____

_____

2. The disciples' question may seem absurd or judgmental to you, but the man's congenital blindness posed a significant theological problem for them. If the man was *born* blind,

did the man actually sin before he was born, as the rabbis erroneously taught, or was it his parents' sin that caused his blindness (Exodus 20:5)?

a. What was unique about Jesus' answer (John 9:3–4)?

_____

_____

_____

_____

b. What do you think is the meaning of the words **day** and **night** (John 9:4)?

_____

_____

_____

3. Some religious teachers believe that all illness and poverty are a result of personal sin or a lack of faith. Proponents of this form of preaching, often known as the "health/wealth prosperity gospel," believe that everyone can be healed of disease and/or be wealthy if he or she simply has enough faith.

a. The Bible teaches that all of us are sinners (Romans 3:10–12). What did Jesus mean when He said **Neither this man nor his parents sinned** (John 9:3)?

_____

_____

b. Name the two churches or groups of churches that were commended for their spiritual richness (faith) even though they were financially poor (2 Corinthians 8:1–5; Revelation 2:8–10).

_____

_____

c. What did the apostle Paul tell the Philippians about faith and suffering (Philippians 1:29)?

_____

_____

_____

d. What did the apostle Peter say about suffering to the believers who had lost everything (1 Peter 1:6–7; 4:12–13)?

_____

_____

_____

4. Jesus told the blind man to go to the Pool of Siloam (which means *sent*) and wash the mud off his eyes (John 9:7). The Pool of Siloam, located in southeastern Jerusalem, is fed by water from the Gihon Spring via an underground aqueduct known as Hezekiah's Tunnel. King Hezekiah originally built the pool as a city water reservoir in the event of a siege. Water for the ceremonies during the Feast of Tabernacles also was drawn from the Pool of Siloam. Why do you think Jesus instructed the man to walk blindly to the pool as opposed to immediately healing him?

_____

_____

_____

_____

_____

5. Jesus' healing of the blind man (the sixth sign) violated rabbinic regulations against kneading clay on the Sabbath. Neighbors and acquaintances of the blind man brought him to the Pharisees for questioning (John 9:8–15). Not satisfied with the blind man's truthful answers, the Pharisees

summoned his parents in order to question them (John 9:18–23). Name at least two mistakes the Pharisees made in their thinking that prevented them from understanding and accepting the truth (John 9:16, 24).

_____

_____

_____

_____

6. The Pharisees held to a strict interpretation of the Old Testament law of Moses and the oral tradition or teachings of eminent Jewish rabbis. History has shown that when "believers" hold to a dual authority—the Word of God and the (religious) teachings of people—they will ultimately choose the human teachings as their higher authority.

    a. If you are a Christian, which is your ultimate spiritual authority: God's Word or the "teachings of man"?

    _____

    _____

    b. What spiritual safeguards have you adopted to prevent yourself (and your family) from being deceived or led astray by religious teachers?

    _____

    _____

    _____

7. The blind man's parents avoided conflict with the Pharisees by encouraging them to reinterview their son (John 9:23). Why were the man's parents so cautious about giving too much information to the religious leaders (John 9:22)?

    _____

    _____

8. a. The blind man demonstrated wisdom and courage as he talked with the Pharisees. Name three things he said in his conversation with the Pharisees that you could use when speaking with someone who is equally close-minded and combative (John 9:25, 30–33).

    _____

    _____

    _____

    _____

It's time to choose your next study. Turn to the back of the study guide for a list of available studies or go online for the latest studies.

ADDITIONAL INSIGHTS

    b. Why were the Pharisees unable to accept the blind man's logical argument (John 9:34)?

    _____

    _____

    _____

    _____

9. Spiritually arrogant and close-minded, the Pharisees refused to allow this "sinner" (the blind man) to challenge their thinking. They **cast him out** of the synagogue (John 9:34; NIV: "threw him out"). What happened next (John 9:35–38)?

    _____

    _____

    _____

    _____

10. At first glance, John 9:39 (**For judgment I have come into this world ...**) appears to contradict John 3:17 (**For God did not send His Son into the world to condemn the world**), and John 12:47 (**for I did not come to judge the world**).

    a. Explain the meaning of Jesus' words in John 9:39.

    _____

    _____

_____

_____

_____

b. Explain the meaning of John 9:41.

_____

_____

_____

ELEVEN

I AM THE GOOD SHEPHERD

Read John 10; other references as given.

Jesus' healing of the blind man fulfilled several Old Testament prophecies and proved He is the Messiah. The blind man received light (physical sight and spiritual salvation), but the Jewish leaders—those who claimed to be spiritually enlightened—remained in darkness. What a paradox!

In John 10, Jesus presents Himself as a good shepherd whose sheep know His voice and follow Him (John 10:1–21). But when Jesus responded to the Jews' pointed question, **If You are the Christ, tell us plainly**, with an undeniable affirmation of His deity (John 10:24), they demonstrated they were not His sheep.

Before you begin, please ask God to reveal Himself through His Word and to give you grace to accept the truths you will be learning.

1. The image of a shepherd and his sheep is steeped in Old Testament theology and biblical culture. Kings and priests were shepherds, and the people were their sheep. Abraham, Isaac, Jacob, and Moses were shepherds. David, also a shepherd, said, **The Lord is my shepherd** (Psalm 23:1). John 10:1–18 is a figure of speech (an allegory). What is an allegory, and what guidelines do you think should be used to correctly interpret one? Use a dictionary if you'd like.

_____

_____

35% Rule:

If the leader talks more than 35% of the time, the group members will be less likely to participate.

———

ADD GROUP INSIGHTS BELOW

_____

_____

_____

_____

2. Every night the shepherds led their flocks into communal sheepfolds, or pens, to protect them from thieves and animals of prey (lions, bears, wolves, etc.). The outer walls of the sheepfolds were constructed of piled stones topped with thorns or briars. A doorkeeper, or watchman (John 10:3), protected the sheep while the shepherds slept. Early each morning the shepherds went to the sheepfold, entered the pen through the door, and called their sheep. The shepherd called his sheep, and they recognized his voice and followed him out to pasture.

   a. Who is the shepherd in John 10:2–4, 11?

   _____

   b. If Jesus is the shepherd, who is the door to the sheepfold?

   _____

   _____

   c. Who do you think are the thieves and robbers (John 10:1, 8) and hirelings (John 10:12; NIV: "hired hand")?

   _____

   _____

   _____

3. In the illustration of the Good Shepherd (Jesus) and His sheep (believers), there is a beautiful picture of how a Christian can learn to walk with Christ.

   a. How does God call His sheep to follow Him (Romans 10:17)?

_____

b. What does it mean to hear Jesus' voice (1 Thessalonians 2:13)?

_____

_____

c. What do you think it means for you to let Jesus lead you as a shepherd (Psalm 23)?

_____

_____

_____

d. Why do the unsaved not hear the Shepherd's (God's) voice (1 Corinthians 1:22–23; 2:14)?

_____

_____

4. Explain how the following individuals respond to the sheep:

a. The thief (John 10:10).

_____

b. The hireling (John 10:12–13).

_____

_____

c. The Good Shepherd (John 10:4, 9–11, 14).

_____

_____

_____

5. The apostle John has presented Jesus as a good Shepherd

It's time to order your next study. Allow enough time to get the books so you can distribute them at the Open House. Consider ordering 2-3 extra books for newcomers.

ADDITIONAL INSIGHTS

(John 10:11). Identify Jesus' two additional shepherding roles, and explain His unique ministry in each of the three (Hebrews 13:20–21; 1 Peter 5:4).

_____

_____

_____

_____

6. When Jesus said **I lay down My life** (John 10:15), He was making reference to His coming crucifixion.

    a. Who do you think are the **other sheep** who will hear His voice and become part of His **one flock** (John 10:16; Ephesians 2:11–18)?

    _____

    _____

    b. List at least two important points Jesus made about His impending death (John 10:17–18).

    _____

    _____

    _____

    _____

7. The Feast of Dedication or Feast of Lights (known today as Hanukkah) commemorates the reconsecration of the temple by Judas Maccabeus in 168 BC, an eight-day celebration in December (**It was winter**, John 10:22).

    a. Why was it that many of the people to whom Jesus spoke could not understand His teachings (John 10:25–27)?

    _____

    _____

ADDITIONAL
INSIGHTS

b. Many people who claim to be Christians seem to have a difficult time hearing (understanding) Jesus. Give at least three reasons why some people are not able to consistently hear from God through His Word (John 10:26–27; Mark 4:17–19).

_____

_____

_____

_____

_____

_____

_____

c. Examine your life before God. Are you consistently able to hear His voice (discern spiritual truth from the lies of this world), and are you following Him to the best of your ability?   Yes / No / Unsure
If not, are you certain you are one of His sheep?

_____

_____

_____

_____

8. What promise did Jesus give His true followers (John 10:28–29)?

_____

_____

_____

9. The Jews asked Jesus to tell them plainly if he was the Christ (John 10:24). They were looking, however, for a self-incriminating confession rather than truth that would lead them to conversion.

a. What was Jesus' answer to their question (John 10:30)?

_____

_____

b. How did the Jewish leaders understand the answer (John 10:33)?

_____

_____

10. The Jews accused Jesus of blasphemy because He told them, in response to their question, that He was God. Then Jesus quoted from Psalm 82:6, which says, **"I said, 'You are gods, ...'"** What point was Jesus trying to make to the Jews (John 10:34–38)? (Note: Here the word "Law" refers to the entire Old Testament, not just the first five Books.)

_____

_____

_____

_____

_____

11. Once again **He [Jesus] escaped out of their hand** (John 10:39) because His time had not yet come. He traveled north along the Jordan River to the place where John (the Baptist) was baptizing. What happened there (John 10:40, 42)?

_____

_____

_____

_____

TWELVE

I AM THE RESURRECTION

Read John 11; other references as given.

Jesus is described as the Word of God, the Lamb of God, the Son of God, the Son of Man, the living water, the Messiah, the true bread of life, the ultimate counselor, the light of the world, the eternal I AM, and the good Shepherd (John 1–10).

In John 11, the apostle John adds another divine attribute to Jesus' impressive profile: He is the resurrection and the life. That glorious truth has brought unspeakable joy to millions of people throughout the ages.

Before you begin, please ask God to reveal Himself through His Word and to give you grace to accept the truths you will be learning.

1. Approximately two miles east of Jerusalem rests the town of Bethany, the home of Jesus' friends Mary, Martha, and Lazarus (John 11:1, 18). When Lazarus (a form of Eleazar) became gravely ill, his two sisters (Mary and Martha) sent word to Jesus about their brother's deteriorating health.

   a. What do Jesus' answer and His delay reveal about His ultimate objective (John 11:4)?

   _____

   _____

Final Exam:

Are you meeting next week to study the Final Exam? To learn how to present it effectively, contact Lamplighters.

———

ADD GROUP INSIGHTS BELOW

b. Has there been a time in your life when God failed to respond to your earnest prayer within your assumed timetable, but later answered in a way that brought more glory to Himself? If so, what spiritual lesson(s) did you learn from that experience?

_____

_____

_____

_____

c. The apostle Paul and others faced a life-threatening situation in Asia, but God ultimately delivered them (2 Corinthians 1:8). What did Paul learn from the experience (2 Corinthians 1:9–10)?

_____

_____

2. After hearing about Lazarus' illness, Jesus delayed two days before going to Bethany (John 11:6). Likely, Mary, Martha, and the rest of their family struggled to understand the reason for His delay.

a. What were the disciples' reactions when Jesus told them they were going to Jerusalem (John 11:8, 16)?

_____

_____

b. What do you think is the meaning of Jesus' illustration about walking during the day and during the night (John 11:9–10)?

_____

_____

_____

_____

3. When Jesus told the disciples that their friend Lazarus was sleeping, they thought He was talking about natural sleep (John 11:11–12). Why did Jesus delay going to Bethany (John 11:15)?

_____

_____

_____

_____

Have you ever thought about discipling another person? It's not hard. Lamplighters offers free Bible study leadership training.

ADDITIONAL INSIGHTS

4. When Mary and Martha sent word to Jesus about their brother's illness, they didn't ask Jesus to come; they simply mentioned that Lazarus was sick. When Jesus met Martha outside of Bethany (John 11:20), Martha said she knew Jesus could request anything in prayer from the Father (John 11:22), but she didn't directly ask Him to resurrect her brother. Knowing her desire, Christ raised Lazarus from the dead. Do you think we believers should follow Martha's example and not come to God with specific requests, knowing that God already knows our hearts, or should we ask God to answer specific prayers? Why?

_____

_____

_____

_____

5. Why do you think Jesus wept when He spoke to Mary about her brother's death—especially when He would shortly thereafter resurrect Lazarus (John 11:32–36, 38)?

_____

_____

_____

_____

6. According to an ancient Jewish tradition, a soul lingered near the body for three days after death in the event the person was revived. Some Bible commentators believe Jesus waited until the fourth day to dispel any intimation that Lazarus had never died.

a. What were the two reactions to this miraculous (seventh) sign (John 11:45–50)?

_____

_____

_____

_____

b. The chief priests and Pharisees acknowledged the miraculous signs Jesus did, but their sin kept them from receiving Him as the Messiah. What was their sin (John 11:47–50)?

_____

_____

_____

7. a. What did the unregenerate High Priest Caiaphas unwittingly prophesy about Jesus Christ's sacrificial death on behalf of the nation of Israel (John 11:49–50)?

_____

_____

b. How did the apostle John interpret Caiaphas' statement about Jesus dying for the nation (John 11:51–52)?

_____

_____

_____

8. The raising of Lazarus forced the Jewish leaders to act. Jesus had to die or they would lose their privileged position with the Romans and religious control over their own people. The Jews' open hostility toward Jesus led Him to travel fifteen miles north to Ephraim, a small town on the edge of the Judean wilderness (John 11:54). Many Bible commentators see a chronological break between John 11:54 and John 11:55. During that intervening time, Jesus taught throughout Perea—the area east of the Jordan, between the Sea of Galilee and the Dead Sea. What notable things occurred during that period (Luke 17:11–21; 18:18–30; 19:1–10)?

_____

_____

_____

_____

_____

_____

9. John 11:55–57 marks the end of this inaugural Lamplighters' study on the gospel of John, but John 11:55 marks the beginning of the end of Jesus' life and ministry. Jesus now was only a few days away from death on the cross. Jewish leaders, anticipating Jesus would attend the Passover celebration, had organized a city-wide manhunt. Anyone who saw Jesus was commanded to report His location so Jewish authorities could seize Jesus and have Him killed (John 11:57).

   a. What are the most important things you learned about Jesus from these first eleven chapters of John?

   _____

   _____

ADDITIONAL
INSIGHTS

b. What did you learn about how an individual receives spiritual truth?

_____

_____

_____

_____

Congratulations! You have just completed a thought-provoking study of John 1–11. I hope you seriously contemplated who Jesus is and what that means to your life. Jesus is God, and He is everything the Bible says He is. Now we encourage you to continue your study in the gospel of John. May the Lord bless you mightily for your diligent study of His precious Word.

Leader's Guide

Lesson 1: Is Jesus Really God?

1. a. Answers will vary. The most common opinions regarding Jesus' identity are: (1) He was a prophet of God akin to Old Testament prophets. (2) A messenger of God, but not divine. (3) He is the sinless Son of God, the Savior of the world (evangelical position). (4) He was a powerful (human) teacher of morality and spirituality who showed man how to live in harmony with others. Other answers could apply.
   b. Answers will vary.

2. a. The phrase refers to the beginning of the time, space, and matter continuum.
   b. Only the Godhead—the Father, the Son (Word), and the Holy Spirit (Spirit of God).

3. a. 1. The Word existed in the beginning before anything else existed except God (John 1:1–2).
      2. The Word was distinct from God (the Father) (John 1:1).
      3. The Word is a person ("He") as distinct from a divine light (New Age), cosmic energy or principle.
      4. The Word was in union with God the Father (John 1:1).
      5. The Word was God yet distinct from God the Father (John 1:1).
      6. The entire heavens and earth were made by the Word (John 1:3).
   b. 1. All things (John 1:3).
      2. Without Him nothing was made (John 1:3).
      3. By Him all things were created that are in heaven and that are on earth (Col. 1:16).
      4. All things were created through Him and for Him (Col. 1:16).

4. The Word is identified as the preexistent Creator God (John 1:1–2). This Word became human (flesh) and dwelt among man on the earth (John 1:14). People beheld His glory—a unique glory that came from God the Father and was only given to the Word (John 1:14). This individual, known only as the Word, also was full of grace and truth (John 1:14). In John

1:17, the One who gave us grace and truth is singularly identified as Jesus Christ. Jesus Christ is the Word.

5. The initial thought may be to see "life" as the physical life God gives man, because the preceding text identifies Jesus as the Creator of all things. This "life," however, was the light of men (John 1:4), which some did not comprehend or accept (John 1:5). Therefore, it is best to understand "life" as the fullness of God's essence, His glorious attributes: holiness, truth, love, omnipotence, sovereignty (William Hendrikson). This "life" includes the physical life Christ gives us, but it also goes far beyond to include all that God originally intended for us in the Garden. This "life," only from Christ and appropriated by man through the gift of salvation, moves man from mere human existence to the abundant life God intended (John 10:10).

6. a. Answers will vary.
    b. Answers will vary.
    c. Answers will vary.

7. a. John's life was to be a witness, to bear witness to the Light, so that through him (John) everyone might believe (John 1:7). John's life purpose pointed others to Christ and to point others away from himself.
    b. John the Baptist's ministry and Christ's call upon the New Testament Christian are remarkably similar. Both men were called to be witnesses and to testify to others that Jesus is the Christ. Both were called to be a voice crying in the wilderness (for John, it was a physical wilderness; for Christians, it is the world that rejects Christ). John sacrificed his life for the advancement of Christ's ministry, and Christians are called to offer their lives as living sacrifices to God (Rom. 12:1).

8. a. Individuals become God's children when they receive Jesus Christ by faith, which means believing in His name (His power to save them, John 1:12). They are born of God, which means He gives them life as a sovereign act of His grace apart from works (John 1:13).
    b. 1. New birth doesn't come from natural/physical descent or parentage (not of bloods, John 1:13).
        2. The new birth does not come from fallen humans' desire or effort. The new birth cannot be accomplished by man's sinful efforts

(however noble they are) because it was man's sinful nature that made it necessary for Christ to die.

3. The new birth does not come from the husband's desire. In John 1:13, the Greek word for "man" often is translated "husband," which is not the same word as in John 1:6. Perhaps a second interpretation of this third disqualifying means of salvation could be "not of human volition whatsoever." The Jews held that because of their "fathers" (their great ancestors) God was obliged to redeem them.

9. Jesus was not part truth and part grace; He was the full embodiment of grace and truth and always conducted Himself in a perfect balance of both. What a powerful example for believers to follow!

Lesson 2: Behold, the Lamb!

1. a. Answers will vary, but should include the following: a conspicuous absence of self-glorification (including boasting, glory-seeking), selfishness, criticism of others, and envy; a conspicuous presence of a sincere concern for the physical, emotional, and spiritual welfare of others manifested in a genuine servant's heart.
   b. Answers will vary.

2. a. 1. John said he was not the Christ (John 1:20).
      2. John said he was not any of the Old Testament prophets (John 1:21).
      3. John said he was only the voice who announced the coming of the Lord: "I am the voice of one crying in the wilderness ..." (John 1:23).
      4. John said Jesus had a higher rank or position in life than he did (John 1:27).
      5. John said he was not worthy even to untie Jesus' sandals (John 1:27, one of the most menial duties of the lowest-ranked servants).
   b. 1. Like Elijah, John the Baptist's ministry burst onto the scene quickly and both their ministries were similar and powerful.
      2. John the Baptist dressed in coarse clothing like Elijah.
      3. The prophet Malachi prophesied that Elijah would return before Messiah's coming (Malachi 4:5). Interestingly, Jesus commended

John the Baptist's ministry and said he was the fulfillment of Malachi's prophecy (Matt. 11:14).

    c. John the Baptist was not the reincarnation of Elijah. Jesus was saying that a prophet similar to Elijah had appeared. In the same way, we might say of a great vocal talent, *"He is Pavarotti."*

3. a. Everything belongs to the Lord, including our lives (Psalm 24:1).
    b. The greatest people of all are those who are the greatest servants of all (Mark 10:44–45).
    c. Man can't do anything without the Lord enabling him (John 15:5).
    d. Everything man has received came from the Lord, so he shouldn't boast as if he gained it by his own abilities and gifting (1 Cor. 4:7).
    e. All man's boasting and glorying should focus on the Lord, not on himself (2 Cor. 10:17).
    f. Believers should actively practice true humility (James 4:10).

4. a. The Lord preserved their lives.
    b. Without spot.

5. Answers will vary.

6. The Lamb of God who takes away the sin of the world (John 1:29). The preexistent Man (John 1:30). The Son of God (John 1:34).

7. a. 1. Information to use to accuse Jesus of wrongdoing (Mark 3:2).
       2. Miraculous signs (Luke 11:29).
       3. God's physical provision and material blessings (John 6:26, 27).
    b. They wanted to see Jesus. Because the Greeks' intended purpose of wanting to see Jesus is not stated, some commentators see their motive as righteous. They were seeking the Lord Himself, not the gifts He could give them.
    c. Answers will vary.

8. a. Andrew said he had found the Messiah.
    b. Phillip said he had found the One whom Moses had written about in the law and the prophets.
    c. Nathaniel believed Jesus was the Son of God, the King of Israel.

9. Jesus becomes the ladder, the means, or stairway, to God (John 1:51).

10. 1. The Word (John 1:1). 2. Christ (John 1:17, 25, 41). 3. The Lamb of God (John 1:29, 36). 4. The Son of God (John 1:34, 49). 5. Rabbi (John 1:38, 49). 6. Messiah (John 1:41). 7. He whom Moses wrote about (John 1:45). 8. Son of Joseph (John 1:45). 9. King of Israel (John 1:49). 10. Son of Man (John 1:51).

Lesson 3: The First Miraculous Sign

1. It was the third day since the call of the first disciples. In that sense, it was the third day since the beginning of Christ's earthly ministry. The numbering of the days according to the call of the first disciples highlights the importance of Jesus' earthly ministry and His work in and through His followers.

2. a. Answers will vary. Mary's subsequent actions (informing the servants to do as Jesus commanded them) suggest that she may have been serving as an assistant to the host or a close friend of the wedding couple. If she was merely a wedding guest, she probably would not have known how much wine was still available. Either way, she was aware of an embarrassing situation, and she turned to Jesus, who she believed could solve the problem and avoid a crisis.

    b. Jesus was communicating to His mother that His ultimate loyalty was to the Father's will from that time forward. Mary had learned a painful lesson earlier in Jesus' life when He said, "Did you not know that I must be about My Father's business?" (Luke 2:49). Now Jesus was making the break official. From that point forward, Jesus would function entirely according to the Father's will and timing.

3. a. Mary was morally pure as a young woman (Luke 1:27).
    b. Mary was highly favored by the Lord and blessed among all women to be the mother of Jesus (Luke 1:28).
    c. Mary was a woman of incredible faith (Luke 1:38). She accepted God's plan for her life without wavering in unbelief.
    d. Mary was a sinner who needed a Savior (Luke 1:47, **my soul rejoices in God my Savior**).
    e. Mary was faithful to Jesus until the end (John 19:25).

4. It is likely that Jesus was so moved with compassion that He was compelled to act. Perhaps He was planning to do so before His mother's request, and His "negative" reply to her pertained to the timing of His action rather than the operation of it. The concept of Jesus' time (has not yet come, the time has come, I have come for this hour) is a powerful theme in John's gospel.

5. a. Jesus instructed the servants to fill the six water pots with water. Then He instructed the servants to draw some out of the water pots and take it to the master of the feast. The servants did as Jesus commanded and the host was the first to recognize the water as wine. The six jars were filled to the brim, leaving no room for wine to be poured in on top. The servants and the host were innocent participants in the miracle, leaving them impartial in their assessment of the jars' contents. The host's comments about the quality of the wine indicate he possessed an acute ability to determine the wine's quality and the clear-mindedness to do so.

    b. John 2:11 indicates turning the water into wine was the first sign. In John's gospel, a sign is a miracle that points people to Jesus. On a subsequent trip to Cana of Galilee, Jesus stayed in the same city where He had turned water into wine (John 4:46).

6. a. Wine and other alcoholic beverages often mock their users (Prov. 20:1). People think they are acting wisely when they are drinking, but the opposite is usually the case. Alcohol consumption often leads to fighting and other forms of conflict and abuse (Prov. 20:1). Those who are led astray by alcohol are playing the fool.

    b. Alcohol consumption often leads to serious trouble (woes), sorrow, arguments, injury, and bloodshot eyes (Prov. 23:29). It can impede users from seeing clearly, causing them to say perverse things, and can distort a person's physical balance (Prov. 23:33–35).

    c. Leaders shouldn't drink lest they make bad decisions as a result of forgetting God's laws (Prov. 31:4–5).

    d. Alcohol can be used for medicinal purposes and as a sedative for those who are dying (Prov. 31:6–7).

7. The first sign revealed (manifested) Jesus' glory, and the disciples believed in Him.

8. a. Jesus made a whip of cords, drove the moneychangers, sheep and oxen out of the temple, poured out the changers' money, and overturned their tables. Then He said, **"Take these things away! Do not make My Father's house a house of merchandise!"**

    b. Rather than repenting of their sin, the Jews asked Jesus to perform a miraculous sign to substantiate His right to do what He had done. They completely missed the point of the object lesson.

9. Jesus knew that a faith in Him that was based on miraculous signs was shallow and fickle. Many of the early followers put their faith in Him for ignoble reasons, and others eventually turned away from Him (John 6:26, 66). For this reason Jesus was not going to commit Himself to them.

Lesson 4: You Must Be Born Again

1. a. Nicodemus thought Jesus was a rabbi (teacher of the Old Testament Law of Moses and the oral Jewish tradition) and a miracle worker who performed miracles through God's power.

    b. *Unless a person is born again, he cannot see the kingdom of God.*

2. a. Nicodemus interpreted Jesus' answer from an entirely natural perspective.

    b. Jesus reiterated the man's need to be born again as a prerequisite for entering the kingdom of God (John 3:5). Next, Jesus explained the distinctiveness of being born of the flesh (the natural birth) and being born of the Spirit (the supernatural birth, or salvation). He then emphasized again the absolutely essential requirement of being born again. Lastly, Jesus acknowledged that being born again is somewhat mysterious (the wind blows wherever it wants), but it is real nevertheless.

    c. Answers will vary.

3. This difficult question has puzzled theologians for centuries — not because there is no plausible answer, but because there are three plausible answers. Some believe # 1 is the right answer because Nicodemus is confused about the new birth as it compares to natural birth. According to this view, Jesus explains the first birth (birth of water) and then the spiritual birth.

John 3:6 seems to explain verse 5. Number 2 seems a little forced, and #3 can be eliminated because it teaches that baptism is necessary for salvation. Number 4 has a strong connection to Old Testament teaching on the new birth (Ezek. 36:24–27) and would have helped Nicodemus connect the two. Number 5 finds its support in the teaching of John the Baptist, who taught water baptism as evidence of genuine repentance. According to this view, Jesus was teaching man's need for repentance and the saving work of the Spirit—both necessary for the new birth to occur.

4. Jesus' answer indicates the concept of new birth is both an Old and New Testament doctrine. Jesus' answer assumed Nicodemus should have known the teaching of the new birth as a teacher of Israel. It also teaches that, even though religious leaders are diligent in their studies of the Word, they can completely miss major doctrinal truths in God's Word. This same phenomenon occurs today when spiritual leaders (elders, pastors, Bible teachers) fail to understand the biblical teaching on new birth.

5. a. 1. In both situations man is incapable of saving himself.
        2. In both situations God provides the remedy for man's sin.
        3. In both situations man must turn to God to be saved from destruction.
        4. In both situations God's provision for man's sin is effective.
    b. Whoever believes in Jesus. This means more than merely a mental belief in Jesus' existence. It means trusting in Christ for eternal life and accepting His free offer of eternal life based on His sacrificial death on man's behalf. Man receives the gift of eternal life solely based on God's sovereign grace, apart from works.
    c. Those who do not believe live under the present judgment of God (**condemned already**, John 3:18) and are excluded from God's presence forever (**perish**, John 3:15).
    d. Man loves darkness rather the light of God (John 3:19). In his natural (unregenerate) state, man hates the light of God because he doesn't want his actions to be exposed or revealed (John 3:20).
    e. Christians should live with a sense of divinely inspired urgency to reach the lost with the message of salvation (John 4:35). They should adapt to the culture they are trying to reach (within the constraints of Scripture) in order to reach nonbelievers with the Gospel (1 Cor. 9:19–22). Christians should realize the horrible fate of those who die

without Christ (they will experience the terror of the Lord's wrath) and do everything they can to reach them for Christ before it is too late (2 Cor. 5:11). Christians should serve as God's ambassadors and work to reconcile the world to Christ by presenting the gospel (2 Cor. 5:20).

6. a. 1. Whatever God has given John and his disciples (followers, spiritual influence, etc.) is a gift from God, and they should be satisfied (John 3:27).
   2. John said he was not the Christ. He (John) was not the main attraction. He was only called to play a support role—one that announced the coming of the Lord (John 3:28).
   3. John said he was the friend of the bridegroom (Christ). As such, his role was to serve Jesus as a loyal friend and rejoice at the sound of His voice (John 3:29). John greatly rejoiced at hearing the voice of Christ, so nothing more needed to be done. John's joy was fulfilled.
   4. Christ and His ministry must increase, and John's ministry was in a state of decline (John 3:30). It was God's plan!
   5. Christ is from heaven, and John was from earth. Jesus naturally would have a superior position (John 3:31).

   b. In the Old Testament period, there was a unique ministry of the Spirit whereby He came upon individuals (prophets, kings, craftsmen) for specific ministries (Judges 3:10; 11:29; Psalm 51:11) and limited times. Jesus, on the other hand, spoke perfect truth because He was given a full measure of the Spirit.

7. They will not see eternal life, and the wrath of God abides on them.

Lesson 5: Total Refreshment

1. a. 1. Jesus was not afraid of potential conflict.
   2. Jesus was willing to go out of His way to reach the lost.
   3. Jesus was willing to cross ethnic barriers to reach the lost.
   4. Jesus expects His followers to risk danger to reach the lost.

   b. Answers will vary.

2. She was a woman, and she was a Samaritan (John 4:9).

3.   a.   1.   Jesus suggested that He knew something she didn't know (**If you knew** ..., John 4:10).
          2.   Jesus used the word "gift" and suggested that she could have this gift (John 4:10).
          3.   Jesus suggested that she didn't know His true identity (John 4:10). He appealed to her natural curiosity.
          4.   Jesus suggested that she should be the one who is asking Him for living water (John 4:10). Since he didn't have a bucket or rope, she must have been intrigued by His offer. Other answers could apply.
     b.   Answers will vary. Knowing how to use well-designed, intriguing spiritual questions is an essential aspect of effective personal evangelism.

4.   a.   Jesus told her that the water from Jacob's Well would not give her total refreshment or lasting satisfaction (John 4:13). She would have to come back regularly to the same well. (In the hot, arid conditions of the Middle East where water is scarce, she could relate well to Jesus' statement.) Jesus also reiterated that He would give this water to her and it would be a fountain springing up to eternal life. The living water Jesus could give her would completely satisfy her forever. What an offer!
     b.   Eternal life with an emphasis on the working of the Holy Spirit in and through the believer's life.

5.   a.   A biblical gospel presentation must deal with the subject of personal sin. Many modern gospel presentations focus on receiving the gift of eternal life without addressing the problem of man's sinfulness in relation to a holy God. In Jesus' interaction with the Samaritan woman, He didn't accuse her of immoral behavior, but He addressed her sinfulness by asking her to call her husband and letting the Holy Spirit bring conviction. Her short, cryptic answer (John 4:17, Gk. *suchi echo andra* – "not I have husband") indicates she was under conviction and she didn't want to talk about her personal life. If the unsaved don't acknowledge their sin before a holy God, either they will not see their need for the Savior, or they could pray a shallow prayer that falls short of true salvation.
     b.   Jesus' response presents another powerful lesson on personal evangelism. He refused to let her catch Him in a religious "denominational" battle (John 4:21, Samaritan versus Jewish). Jesus told her it was not

about where someone worshipped, but about *Who* they worshipped (the Savior) and *how* they worshipped (in spirit and in truth).

6. Worshipping in spirit means an individual offers himself so completely in adoration and praise to God that God's glory is his sole and objective desire. Worshipping in truth means an individual offers himself in full harmony with the truth of God as revealed in His Word. Both aspects of worship must be present in order to worship in spirit and in truth.

7. a. Now was the time for the harvest of souls. They were not to be complacent or indolent in the duty of reaching the lost. They were to lift up their eyes (gain a more eternal perspective) and begin to see the spiritual opportunities all around them. The phrase "white for harvest" means people are ready to be saved *now!*
    b. Many came to Christ (John 4:41).

8. a. From a human perspective, it often takes the testimony and spiritual influence of more than one person to bring someone to salvation (John 4:36–38).
    b. Believers are commanded to pray for God to raise up more laborers because the harvest is great. The problem is not with the harvest, but with the lack of harvesters (Matt. 9:37–38).
    c. For most believers, effectiveness at personal evangelism is something that is learned (Mark 1:17).

9. a. Jesus healed an individual at a different location.
    b. Since Jesus doesn't need to be physically present, a believer should be encouraged to pray to Him, knowing that He has the power to answer his or her prayers.

Lesson 6: Is Jesus Equal With God?

1. a. "Do you want to be made well?"
    b. The paralytic came regularly to the pool. His immediate response to Jesus indicated that he had not lost hope even though he had not yet been healed.

2. a. No major doctrine in the Bible is in question as a result of the textual variants.

    b. The doctrine of biblical inerrancy applies to the original Hebrew, Aramaic, and Greek manuscripts from which all translations derive their authority. Most differences in translations are due to translation style (modified literal, dynamic equivalence, paraphrase), not the ancient manuscripts.

3. a. 1. God wants us to show compassion to all people, including those of other ethnicities and nationalities (Luke 10:30–37).

       2. God's people should not assume sickness or health-related problems are a direct result of someone's sin (John 9:1–3).

       3. Christians should realize that sicknesses could be the result of sin in a believer's life (1 Cor. 11:27–30). Christians should not judge why another person is sick, but they should be aware of the possibility and help the individual recognize that sin could be a contributing factor.

       4. Christians should be willing to pray for those who are sick (James 5:14–16). They should also encourage the sick person to seek medical help (anointing him with oil).

    b. Paul viewed them as a direct intervention by God, as an opportunity to receive more of God's grace and be strengthened by His power, and as an opportunity to bring glory to God.

4. The Jews were openly critical (John 5:10). They were more concerned about Who healed the man than that the man had been healed (John 5:12). They sought to persecute Jesus and kill Him (John 5:16).

5. a. 1. We become hyper-critical toward others (Mark 7:2).

       2. We focus on minor issues and make them major issues with others (Mark 7:5).

       3. We become hypocrites, honoring God with our lips while our hearts are far from Him (Mark 7:6).

       4. We worship God in vain (Mark 7:7).

       5. We become confused about what is true, and we teach as truth religious "doctrines of man" (Mark 7:7).

       6. We devalue God's Word so we can promote the teachings of men (Mark 7:9). In doing so, we reject God's Word in order to keep our man-made religious traditions.

b. Answers will vary.

6. 1. Jesus, like the Father, works every day (John 5:17; Psalm 121:3–4).
   2. Jesus is equal with God the Father (John 5:17–18).
   3. Jesus lived in full communion with the Father (John 5:19–20). He never acted independently of the Father's will. Whatever the Father showed Jesus, He did.
   4. Jesus has the power to resurrect others to life (John 5:21).
   5. All future eternal judgment has been committed to Jesus (John 5:22–23) so that everyone will ultimately honor Him, either in salvation or judgment (John 5:25–30).

7. a. 1. John the Baptist (John 5:32–35).
      2. Jesus' works (John 5:36).
      3. God the Father (John 5:37–38).
      4. The (OT) Scriptures (John 5:39).
   b. They focused on the minutiae of the Word and missed the big picture — the person of Jesus Christ.
   c. Believers need to realize that God wants them to have a relationship with His Son, not just with a book. The Christian's relationship with God shouldn't be reduced to principles, promises, and prohibitions. The believer cannot know Christ without knowing His Word, but the Christian's religious experience will become cold and sterile if he never sees Christ in the Scriptures.

8. They didn't have the love of God in them (John 5:42), and they were more concerned about their religious standing among religious peers than pleasing God (John 5:44).

9. a. The Old Testament Law of Moses condemned their actions. For example, the sixth commandment says, **You shall not murder** (Exod. 20:13), but the Jews were planning to kill Jesus. Jesus said they were trusting Moses (at least that's what the Jews claimed) even though they weren't.
   b. Jesus said the Old Testament is filled with images and references to Himself.

Lesson 7: I AM the Bread of Life

1. a. Answers will vary. God tests His people to reveal Himself and His power and to give them an opportunity to trust Him.
    b. Answers will vary.

2. a. The Merriam-Webster dictionary defines a miracle as an extraordinary event manifesting divine intervention in human affairs. A miracle could also be defined as God intervening in the laws of nature to reveal His glory and power.
    b. Some thought Jesus was the Prophet who was to come into the world. There was the expectation that a notable figure (the Prophet) would come, and many thought Jesus was the fulfillment of the ancient prophecy. Others wanted to make Jesus their earthly king.
    c. Jesus left the superficial crowd and went alone to a mountainside.

3. The disciples didn't learn anything from the miracle of the feeding of the five thousand because their hearts were hardened.

4. a. Jesus said that the people followed Him, not because of the signs He did, but because He fed them.
    b. The only "work" man can do that is pleasing to Him is to believe in Him.
    c. It seems as though the people didn't hear what Jesus had just told them. They asked Him for another sign so they could believe in Him.

5. a. It was God, not Moses, who provided the Israelites with manna in the wilderness (John 6:32).
    b. The bread of God is not physical food, but a Person who comes down from heaven (John 6:33).
    c. The bread of God gives life, not just temporary nutrition (John 6:33).
    d. The bread of God gives life to the world, not just physical bread to one nation (John 6:33).

6. a. Those who come to Christ will never experience spiritual longing (John 6:35, never hunger or thirst).
    b. All those who have been called by the Father come to Christ (John 6:37).

c.	All those who come to Christ are accepted (John 6:37).

d.	Jesus came to earth to do the Father's will. We all can be certain that there are not two agendas—Jesus' and the Father's (John 6:38).

e.	Everyone who has been redeemed (**all He has given me**) will be resurrected (John 6:39).

f.	It is God's will that everyone who believes will have everlasting life (John 6:40).

7.	a.	No one can come to Christ unless the Father draws him (John 6:44). And everyone who has heard and learned from the Father comes to Christ (John 6:44–45).

b.	Man must believe (trust in Christ alone) for eternal life (John 6:47).

8.	Man is depraved and estranged from God and wants nothing to do with Him (John 3:19–20). Not only is man unwilling to come to God, he is totally incapable of coming to God (1 Corinthians 2:14; 2 Corinthians 4:4). God calls men through the convicting power of the Holy Spirit and the Word of God. Those who are convicted of their sin and convinced about the true identity of Jesus Christ by the power of the Holy Spirit are given faith to believe. Those who respond to God's call (the elect) are redeemed and sealed in Christ forever.

9.	a.	In John 6:2 the Bible says that many followed Jesus because of the signs He performed. Jesus rebuked shallow followers for their superficial level of faith (John 6:53–58) by saying that unless they ate His flesh and drank His blood, the shallow carnival-following crowd would not be saved. Jesus was telling them that they needed to accept Him fully in order to be saved.

b.	Many of Jesus' disciples thought His teaching on this subject was hard. Obviously, they didn't accept the part they didn't understand (John 6:60–61). Many of Jesus' disciples stopped following Him after that time (John 6:66).

10. Answers will vary.

Lesson 8: Life's Most Important Question

1.	Jesus' brothers wanted Him to go up to Jerusalem to the Feast of

Tabernacles, perhaps because they knew many of His disciples had left and they viewed the feast as a good opportunity to regain more followers. Even though Jesus' brothers were nonbelievers, it is likely they were enamored by His popularity and took pride in being related to Him.

2. a. 1. Christians should seek the Lord through His Word (Judges 18:5).
        2. Believers will have peace (the presence of the Lord) if they are following the Lord's will (Judges 18:6).
        3. Believers should trust in the Lord with all their hearts and not trust only in their own reasoning (Proverbs 3:5).
        4. Believers should seek the counsel of other godly believers (Proverbs 11:14).
        5. Believers should dedicate themselves as living sacrifices to God, resist the temporal values of this world, and allow their minds to be transformed by God's Word (Romans 12:1–2).
    b. The second aspect of fulfilling God's will is the timing. Often it is easy to know what God wants but more difficult to sense God's leading in the execution of His will.

3. The Jewish people wanted to know where Jesus was (John 7:11). There was a lot of complaining (or grumbling) about Jesus (John 7:12). Some thought He was a good man, but others thought he was a deceiver (John 7:12). Others marveled at Jesus' wisdom, knowing he had not attended a rabbinic school (John 7:15). There were also those who thought He was demon-possessed (John 7:20).

4. a. 1. They don't want their sins to be exposed so they hide from the truth (John 3:19–20).
        2. They don't have the capacity or ability to understand the truth because they have never been born again. The Holy Spirit (the Spirit of Truth; John 16:13) is the One who guides man into an understanding of the truth, and the Spirit is not present in the lives of the unsaved.
    b. An individual cannot receive anything unless it is given to him from heaven (God).
    c. Before he can consistently understand and discern spiritual truth, man must desire to do God's will.

5. Circumcision was performed on the eighth day after birth. If the eighth day had fallen on the Sabbath, the child still would be circumcised on that day. Jesus used the rite of circumcision, performed on the eighth day, as an example of partial healing and compared it to the complete healing of the paralytic to show the inconsistency of their thinking. Jesus argued that if it was right to circumcise a child on the eighth day, then why wasn't it also right to heal someone else on the Sabbath? Note: Regarding the circumcision of the male children on the eighth day, Professor H. Dam discovered that vitamin K helps prevent hemorrhaging. Vitamin K is responsible for the production of prothrombin. If there is a vitamin K deficiency, there will also be a prothrombin deficiency, and hemorrhaging may occur. Interestingly, it is only on the 5th to the 7th days of the newborn male's life that vitamin K is present in adequate quantities. Since vitamin K is not produced in sufficient quantities until days five through seven and the amount of prothrombin present is elevated above 100% on the eighth day, it is the only day in the male's life in which this will be the case under normal conditions. If surgery (circumcision) is to be performed, day eight is the perfect day to do it.

6. a. Some thought Jesus may be the Christ, but they weren't sure (John 7:25–26). Others believed in Him but didn't fully understand who He was (John 7:31). These interesting verses teach that people can believe in Christ but their faith falls short of salvation. Some thought Jesus was the Prophet to come, while others thought He was the Christ (John 7:40–41). The chief priests and Pharisees thought Jesus was merely a man (John 7:46).
    b. Answers will vary.
    c. Jesus was referring to His coming crucifixion and resurrection and to His entrance into heaven. It could also be a veiled reference to the chief priests' and Pharisees' inability to locate Jesus' body after the crucifixion (Matthew 28:11–15).

7. a. There has to be a spiritual thirst (established by the Holy Spirit as the person is convicted of sin) and genuine faith in Christ (John 7:38).
    b. The Living Water is identified as the indwelling Holy Spirit, working in and through the redeemed person.

8. a. Spiritual arrogance and pride.

    b.   Nicodemus thought there should be a fair trial that would honestly judge the merits of Christ. The Pharisees had already condemned Jesus in their minds.

    c.   Answers will vary.

Lesson 9: I AM the Light of the World

1.   Answers will vary.

2.   a.   When counseling someone caught in sin, the first thing to do is eliminate the voice of the accusers. This helps the accused focus on the counseling that can help them.

    b.   The second thing to do is assure the counselee that you are there to help them, not to accuse or hurt them. This helps the accused relax and begin to trust you.

3.   a.   The third thing to do is to give the counselee confidence that they can overcome their sin. Their sin doesn't need to keep destroying them. For Christians, the power to overcome sin comes from Christ alone (1 Corinthians 10:13).

    b.   Answers will vary.

4.   The world (not the earth, but the entire realm of man) is under the dominion of Satan who negatively influences the minds and values of fallen humanity (2 Corinthians 4:4). The Bible uses the word *darkness* to describe the sin, evil, and ignorance of this system and its unwitting subjects. Jesus is the light (not *a* light) who enables man to see through the deception and delusion of this fallen world and its distorted values and gives him truth to overcome the darkness. If an individual follows Christ (salvation, sanctification), he will receive the light needed to live successfully and will never stumble (walk in darkness). That doesn't mean he will not experience trouble; it means he will always have sufficient truth to guide him through trials.

5.   The religious leaders rejected this truth.

6.   a.   Those without Christ will die in their sin (John 8:21). Their sin (singular) is the sin of unbelief.

    b.   Those without Christ will not be allowed into heaven (John 8:21).

   c. Those without Christ are "of this world," meaning their values, priorities, and perspective in life are immersed in the world's value system (John 8:23).

   d. Those without Christ will be judged for their sins (John 8:24). Their specific sins (plural) will be revealed in judgment (Revelation 20:11–15).

7. a. If they abide in His Word, they are truly His disciples (John 8:31). Then He promised those who believed in Him that the Word would set them free (John 8:32).

   b. To abide in the Word of Christ means to make the Word of God the ultimate authority in everything a person believes and does. It means continually surrendering thoughts and feelings that are contrary to God's Word and embracing the truth regardless of human reasoning and feelings. It means doing what God has commanded regardless of the consequences to us.

   c. Answers will vary.

8. a. Those who practice sin are slaves of sin (John 8:34). Just as a slave in a household does not live in the house forever, so are those who habitually sin do not experience the fellowship of God in their lives.

   b. God set us free at salvation from the slavery to sin (Romans 6:17–18). Believers are called slaves of righteousness (Romans 6:18), but they must present their members (minds, eyes, etc.) to God's purposes to fulfill His mission (Romans 6:19–20). Before a believer was saved he reaped a harvest of death (Romans 6:21), but now he can reap holiness and eternal life (Romans 6:21–22).

9. Jesus said that if God were their father, they would love Him (Christ). But because their father is the devil (and he is a murderer and a liar), they cannot accept the truth.

10. a. He will not experience the second or eternal death – separation from God.

   b. The Jews understood Jesus to be saying he was greater than Abraham, who died. The Jews mocked Him and thought He was insane.

11. a. Jesus said, **Most assuredly, I say to you, before Abraham was, I AM.**

b. He was saying He was God, the Jehovah or Yahweh of the Old Testament. This was an undeniable claim to deity.

Lesson 10: The Messianic Miracle

1. The disciples wanted to know if the man's blindness was caused by his parents' sin or his own. The man had been born blind, and the question of congenital blindness confused them.

2. a. Jesus said the man's blindness was not a result of sin, either his or his parents'. The man's physical handicap, Jesus said, occurred so that the works of God (the miraculous healing) might be demonstrated or revealed. Jesus also said He must work while it was still day (the opportunity to do good regardless of what day it was) because the time was coming when no one could work (the end of the world).
    b. "Day" refers to the period of time Jesus had to accomplish the work given to Him by the Father. "Night" refers to the time when that work would be complete.

3. a. This verse doesn't mean that neither the man nor his parents had ever sinned. It means the man's blindness was not caused by a direct sinful act either by his parents or himself.
    b. The churches of Macedonia (2 Corinthians 8:1–5). The church in Smyrna (Revelation 2:8–10).
    c. Paul told the Philippians that God had granted them the dual privileges of being saved and suffering for the cause of Christ (Philippians 1:29).
    d. Peter told them to rejoice even though they were experiencing fiery trials, because the trials would reveal the genuineness of their faith and God would reward them with praise, honor, and glory when Christ returns.

4. Jesus performed a wide array of healing miracles. Some were performed instantaneously without any faith on the part of the recipient. Others required an act of faith by the person being healed. Some were children, others adults. The full array of Jesus' miracles revealed the extent of His power and glory. In the case of the man born blind, perhaps his walking a considerable distance helped more people remember that he was blind before he received his sight. Other answers could apply.

5. a. The Pharisees were prejudicial in their thinking. Their statement, "This man," indicates their minds were made up. To them, Jesus was only a man, nothing more. When they interrogated with such a degree of prejudice, they could only reach limited conclusions; their own.
    b. The Pharisees didn't know the Word of God. Jesus hadn't violated the Sabbath; He had violated the rabbis' interpretation of the Old Testament. This is a classic example of how man-made religious traditions can supersede true teachings of the Word of God.

6. a. Answers will vary.
    b. Answers will vary, but could include the following: reading the Bible daily, being an active part of a Bible-believing church, avoiding religious teachers who offer a steady stream of topical messages or who don't teach the Bible in context, and avoiding religious teachers who are extremists or who isolate their followers.

7. The blind man's parents didn't want to be put out of the synagogue (John 9:22).

8. a. 1. He demonstrated humility (**Whether He is a sinner or not, I do not know**). 2. He spoke with conviction about his personal experience (**One thing I know: that though I was blind, now I see**). 3. He used clear, rational arguments when he questioned the Pharisees about how God could use a sinner to open a blind man's eyes (John 9:30, 33).
    b. The Pharisees were spiritually arrogant. They saw the blind man as a sinner and themselves as righteous. Their theology was faulty because they saw the man's blindness as a result of his sin prior to birth.

9. Jesus heard the man had been cast out of the synagogue and found him (John 9:35). When Jesus asked him if he believed in the Son of God, the man was saved (John 9:37–38).

10. a. Jesus' main purpose for coming into the world the first time was to bring salvation (Luke 19:10; John 3:17). The Jews' rejection, however, brought judgment upon themselves. Jesus said the Jewish leaders would be judged because they claimed to see (John 9:39, 41).
    b. If the Pharisees were blind to spiritual truth, they could claim ignorance. But because they claimed they were spiritually enlightened, they were culpable.

Lesson 11: I AM the Good Shepherd

1. The discourse about the good Shepherd is called an illustration (John 10:6; Gk. *paroimia* – literally, wayside saying). It is an allegory rather than a parable. An allegory is like a metaphor in the sense that there is an *implied* comparison (*tell that fox,* meaning Herod); a parable is like a simile in which there is an *expressed* comparison (*his appearance was like* …). A biblical allegory teaches spiritual truth by means of symbolic fictional figures and truths about human existence. Students of the Bible should interpret allegories with great caution. They should not allow the allegory to teach more than the original author intended and not attempt to assign meanings to each aspect of the allegory.

2. a. Jesus Christ (John 10:11).
    b. Jesus Christ is also the door (John 10:9). This dual role (Jesus as shepherd and door) is unusual for an allegory.
    c. The false religious teachers (Jewish scribes, Pharisees, Sadducees) who attempt to pillage the sheep and use them for their own advancement.

3. a. God speaks to us through the Word of God (Romans 10:17).
    b. It means to accept it for what it truly is—the very Word of God and not the words of man. It means to believe it and to allow it to work in and through your life by faith.
    c. It means to acknowledge His leadership in every aspect of our lives, trusting Him to lead us in a good path (still waters), provide for us, and be our defender in times of trial and difficulty.
    d. The gospel is foolishness to the unsaved (Gentiles, 1 Corinthians 1:23) because they are not able to understand God's Word until He reveals it to them (1 Corinthians 2:14).

4. a. The thief comes to kill, steal, and destroy the sheep (John 10:10).
    b. The hireling (NIV: hired man) abandons the sheep in the face of danger (John 10:12–13).
    c. The good Shepherd loves the sheep. The sheep know His voice, and they follow Him (John 10:4). The shepherd leads the sheep out to pasture (John 10:4), and He leads them into the pen where they will have rest and safety (John 10:10). The good Shepherd is willing to lay

down His life for His sheep (John 10:11). The good Shepherd knows His sheep (John 10:14).

5. John 10:11 – As the Good Shepherd, Jesus gave His life for his sheep (those who have been saved).
    Heb. 13:20, 21 – As the Great Shepherd, Jesus sanctifies us through His blood and perfects in us what is well-pleasing to God to bring Him glory.
    1 Peter 5:4 – As the Chief Shepherd, Jesus will return to reward spiritual leaders (elders) who have faithfully shepherded His sheep. The sheep are called the flock of God (1 Peter 5:2) and the elders serve as overseers. They are never the elder's sheep.

6. a. The Gentiles who eventually would be redeemed and made part of God's flock.
    b. 1. God the Father loved Jesus because He was willing to lay down His life (John 10:17).
        2. Jesus had the power to lay down His life and to take it up again (John 10:17–18).

7. a. The Jews (John 10:24) were not Christ's sheep (John 10:26). Only Jesus' sheep can recognize His voice and follow Him. Other sheep— those who are not His own—don't recognize His voice and cannot follow Him.
    b. 1. Those who do not belong to Jesus (the unsaved) can't hear His voice and follow Him (John 10:27).
        2. Those who are weak in the faith may turn back to the world when they face tribulation and persecution for their faith (Mark 4:17).
        3. Those who are worldly-minded turn back to the world because they care too much for riches and other material things (Mark 4:18–19).
    c. Answers will vary.

8. Those who are genuinely redeemed will never perish (spend eternity in the lake of fire). No one is able to snatch them out of Jesus' hand or the Father's hand because He is greater than everyone else (John 10:28–29).

9. a. Jesus and His Father were exactly the same in essence.
    b. The Jews understood Jesus to be saying He was God (John 10:33).

10. Jesus quotes from Psalm 82:6 to prove that referring to Himself as God should not be foreign to their thinking. In Psalm 82 the psalmist used the word *elohim*, a word often translated as God, to refer to Israel's judges. Jesus' point: If the Law used the word *elohim* to refer to men who were merely appointed as human judges, why shouldn't He use the same designation without being accused of blasphemy?

11. Jesus stayed there a while and many people believed in Him. Interestingly, the Apostle John mentioned that the people believed in Him apart from signs.

Lesson 12: I AM the Resurrection

1. a. Jesus' ultimate goal in life was to glorify the Father. He did not heal everyone He met, and He didn't meet every need, physical or emotional. He functions entirely according to a divine plan.
   b. Answers will vary.
   c. Paul learned to trust God more and trust his own strength less (2 Cor. 1:9). He also learned to trust God in the future (2 Cor. 1:10, **He will still deliver us**).

2. a. The disciples were keenly aware that Jesus could die if He went to Jerusalem (John 11:8).
   b. Jesus was saying there was a time to fulfill God's will and that He must be about His Father's business. He could not allow the fear of death to interfere with accomplishing the Father's will. If Jesus walked in the day, He could be sure that He would never stumble (in relationship to doing God's will) regardless of what happened to Him. On the contrary, those who are not walking in God's will inevitably stumble (in their obedience to God) because they don't have the light of God in them.

3. Jesus wanted the disciples to see Lazarus' resurrection so they would believe. The disciples needed to witness a resurrection just prior to Jesus' own death and resurrection so they could have more faith in Christ once He was crucified.

4. Many people in the Scriptures made specific requests of the Lord (Moses, Gideon, David, Nehemiah, Paul). Jesus also offered specific requests to

the Father (John 17:1, 9, 20). Believers should make their requests known to God, but they also must leave the results to Him.

5. The text doesn't indicate why Jesus wept, and commentator speculations abound. We can be sure that Jesus was not weeping for Lazarus, who was about to be raised from the dead. Nor was Jesus weeping for Mary and Martha, who were about to receive their brother back from the grave. It also seems unlikely that Jesus was weeping about the unbelief of the people who were present because they didn't believe he would raise Lazarus. Perhaps Jesus, knowing His crucifixion was near, was weeping because He saw the effects of sin and was emotionally touched by the pain it caused. The Greek word for "wept" (*erchou*) in John 11:35 is not the same as the word for "weep" in verse 11:33. "Wept" in verse 11:33 means to burst into tears.

6. a. Some of the Jews turned to Christ in faith (John 11:45). Some went to the Pharisees to report what He had done (John 11:46). The Pharisees were bewildered and expressed fear that their position with the Roman government might be taken away from them (John 11:47–48). Caiaphas said Jesus must die (John 11:49–50).
   b. They were more concerned about their spiritual standing in Israel than in embracing the truth.

7. a. The high priest said that it was expedient that one should die for the (Jewish) people. This would be better than the whole nation perishing.
   b. The apostle John said Caiaphas didn't really understand what he was saying when he spoke those words, but the Lord directed him to prophesy that Christ would die for Israel and for others who would also become children of God (John 11:52).

8. a. Jesus healed ten leapers at one time, but only one came back to thank Him (Luke 17:11-21).
   b. Jesus had a conversation with the rich young ruler, and the apostles wanted to know who could be saved (Luke 18:18–30).
   c. Zacchaeus, a chief tax gatherer, was led to salvation (Luke 19:1–10).

9. a. Answers will vary.
   b. Answers will vary.

John 1–11: Son of God

FINAL EXAM

Every person will eventually stand before God in judgment—the final exam. The Bible says, **And it is appointed for men to die once, but after this the judgment** (Hebrews 9:27).

May I ask you a question? *If you died today, do you know for certain you would go to heaven?* I did not ask if you're religious or a church member, nor did I ask if you've had some encounter with God—a meaningful spiritual experience. I didn't even ask if you believe in God or angels or if you're trying to live a good life. The question I *am* asking is this: *If you died today, do you know for certain you would go to heaven?*

When you die, you will stand alone before God in judgment. You'll either be saved for all eternity, or you will be separated from God for all eternity in what the Bible calls the lake of fire (Romans 14:12; Revelation 20:11–15). Tragically, many religious people who believe in God are not going to be accepted by Him when they die.

> **Many will say to Me in that day, "Lord, Lord, have we not prophesied in Your name, cast out demons in Your name, and done many wonders in Your name?" And then I will declare to them, "I never knew you; depart from Me, you who practice lawlessness!"** (Matthew 7:22–23)

God loves you and wants you to go to heaven (John 3:16; 2 Peter 3:9). If you are not sure where you'll spend eternity, you are not prepared to meet God. God wants you to know for certain that you will go to heaven.

> **Behold, now is the accepted time; behold, now is the day of salvation.** (2 Corinthians 6:2)

The words **behold** and **now** are repeated because God wants you to know that you can be saved today. You do not need to hear those terrible words, **Depart from Me ....** Isn't that great news?

Jesus himself said, **You must be born again** (John 3:7). These aren't the words of a pastor, a church, or a particular denomination. They're the words of Jesus Christ himself. You *must* be born again (saved from eternal damnation) before you die; otherwise, it will be too late when you die! You can know for certain today that God will accept you into heaven when you die.

110

These things I have written to you who believe in the name of the Son of God, that you may know *that you have eternal life.*

(1 John 5:13)

The phrase **you may know** means that you can know for certain before you die that you will go to heaven. To be born again, you must understand and accept four essential spiritual truths. These truths are right from the Bible, so you know you can trust them—they are not man-made religious traditions. Now, let's consider these four essential spiritual truths.

Essential Spiritual Truth

#1

The Bible teaches that you are a sinner and separated from God.

No one is righteous in God's eyes. To be righteous means to be totally without sin, not even a single act.

There is none righteous, no, not one;
There is none who understands;
There is none who seeks after God.
They have all turned aside;
They have together become unprofitable;
There is none who does good, no, not one.
(Romans 3:10–12)

...for all have sinned and fall short of the glory of God.
(Romans 3:23)

Look at the words God uses to show that all men are sinners—**none**, **not one**, **all turned aside**, **not one**. God is making a point: all of us are sinners. No one is good (perfectly without sin) in His sight. The reason is sin.

Have you ever lied, lusted, hated someone, stolen anything, or taken God's name in vain, even once? These are all sins.

Are you willing to admit to God that you are a sinner? If so, then tell Him right now you have sinned. You can say the words in your heart or aloud—it doesn't matter which—but be honest with God. Now check the box if you have just admitted you are a sinner.

☐   God, I admit I am a sinner in Your eyes.

Spiritual Death

Eternal Life

Now, let's look at the second essential spiritual truth.

Essential Spiritual Truth

#2

The Bible teaches that you cannot save yourself or earn your way to heaven.

Man's sin is a very serious problem in the eyes of God. Your sin separates you from God, both now and for all eternity—unless you are born again.

For the wages of sin is death.
(Romans 6:23)

And you He made alive, who were dead in trespasses and sins.
(Ephesians 2:1)

Wages are a payment a person earns by what he or she has done. Your sin has earned you the wages of death, which means separation from God. If you die never having been born again, you will be separated from God after death.

You cannot save yourself or purchase your entrance into heaven. The Bible says that man is **not redeemed with corruptible things, like silver or gold** (1 Peter 1:18). If you owned all the money in the world, you still could not buy your entrance into heaven. Neither can you buy your way into heaven with good works.

For by grace you have been saved through faith, and that not of yourselves; it is the gift of God, not of works, lest anyone should boast. (Ephesians 2:8–9)

The Bible says salvation is **not of yourselves**. It is **not of works, lest anyone should boast**. Salvation from eternal judgment cannot be earned by doing good works; it is a gift of God. There is nothing you can do to purchase your way into heaven because you are already unrighteous in God's eyes.

If you understand you cannot save yourself, then tell God right now that you are a sinner, separated from Him, and you cannot save yourself. Check the box below if you have just done that.

☐ God, I admit that I am separated from You because of my sin. I realize that I cannot save myself.

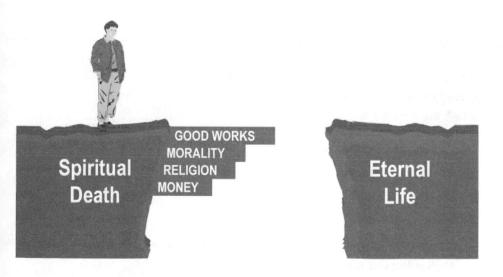

Now, let's look at the third essential spiritual truth.

Essential Spiritual Truth

#3

The Bible teaches that Jesus Christ died on the cross to pay the complete penalty for your sin and to purchase a place in heaven for you.

Jesus Christ, the sinless Son of God, lived a perfect life, died on the cross, and rose from the dead to pay the penalty for your sin and purchase a place in heaven for you. He died on the cross on your behalf, in your place, as your substitute, so you do not have to go to hell. Jesus Christ is the only acceptable substitute for your sin.

For He [God, the Father] made Him [Jesus] who knew [committed] no sin to be sin for us, that we might become the righteousness of God in Him.
(2 Corinthians 5:21)

I [Jesus] am the way, the truth, and the life. No one comes to the Father except through Me.
(John 14:6)

Nor is there salvation in any other, for there is no other name under heaven given among men by which we must be saved.
(Acts 4:12)

Jesus Christ is your only hope and means of salvation. Because you are a sinner, you cannot pay for your sins, but Jesus paid the penalty for your sins by dying on the cross in your place. Friend, there is salvation in no one else—not angels, not some religious leader, not even your religious good works. No religious act such as baptism, confirmation, or joining a church can save you. There is no other way, no other name that can save you. Only Jesus Christ can save you. You must be saved by accepting Jesus Christ's substitutionary sacrifice for your sins, or you will be lost forever.

Do you see clearly that Jesus Christ is the only way to God in heaven? If you understand this truth, tell God that you understand, and check the box below.

☐ God, I understand that Jesus Christ died to pay the penalty for my sin. I understand that His death on the cross was the only acceptable sacrifice for my sin.

Essential Spiritual Truth

#4

By faith, you must trust in Jesus Christ alone for eternal life and call upon Him to be your Savior and Lord.

Many religious people admit they have sinned. They believe Jesus Christ died for the sins of the world, but they are not saved. Why? Thousands of moral, religious people have never completely placed their faith in Jesus Christ *alone* for eternal life. They think they must believe in Jesus Christ as a real person and do good works to earn their way to heaven. They are not trusting Jesus Christ alone. To be saved, you must trust in Jesus Christ *alone* for eternal life. Look what the Bible teaches about trusting Jesus Christ alone for salvation.

> *Believe on the Lord Jesus Christ, and you will be saved.*
> (Acts 16:31)

> *...that if you confess with your mouth the Lord Jesus and believe in your heart that God has raised Him from the dead, you will be saved. For with the heart one believes unto righteousness, and with the mouth confession is made unto salvation.... For there is no distinction between Jew and Greek, for the same Lord over all is rich to all who call upon Him. For "whoever calls on the name of the Lord shall be saved.*
> (Romans 10:9–10, 12–13)

Do you see what God is saying? To be saved or born again, you must trust Jesus Christ *alone* for eternal life. Jesus Christ paid for your complete salvation. Jesus said, **It is finished!** (John 19:30). Jesus paid for your salvation completely when He shed His blood on the cross for your sin.

If you believe that God resurrected Jesus Christ (proving God's acceptance of Jesus as a worthy sacrifice for man's sin) and you are willing to confess Jesus Christ as your Savior and Lord (master of your life), you will be saved.

Friend, right now God is offering you the greatest gift in the world. God wants to give you the *gift* of eternal life, the *gift* of His complete forgiveness for all your sins, and the *gift* of His unconditional acceptance into heaven when you die. Will you accept His free gift now, right where you are?

Are you unsure how to receive the gift of eternal life? Let me help you. Do you remember that I said you needed to understand and accept four essential spiritual truths? First, you admitted you are a sinner. Second, you admitted you were separated from God because of your sin and you could not save yourself. Third, you realized that Jesus Christ is the only way to heaven—no other name can save you.

Now, you must trust that Jesus Christ died once and for all to save your lost soul. Just take God at His word—He will not lie to you! This is the kind of simple faith you need to be saved. If you would like to be saved right now, right where you are, offer this prayer of simple faith to God. Remember, the words must come from your heart.

God, I am a sinner and deserve to go to hell. Thank You, Jesus, for dying on the cross for me and for purchasing a place in heaven for me. I believe You are the Son of God and You are able to save me right now. Please forgive me for my sin and take me to heaven when I die. I invite You into my life as Savior and Lord, and I trust You alone for eternal life. Thank You for giving me the gift of eternal life. Amen.

If, in the best way you know how, you trusted Jesus Christ alone to save you, then God just saved you. He said in His Holy Word, ***But as many as received Him, to them He gave the right to become the children of God*** (John 1:12). It's that simple. God just gave you the gift of eternal life by faith. You have just been born again, according to the Bible.

You will not come into eternal judgment, and you will not perish in the lake of fire—you are saved forever! Read this verse carefully and let it sink into your heart.

> ***Most assuredly, I say to you, he who hears My word and believes in Him who sent Me has everlasting life, and shall not come into judgment, but has passed from death into life.***
> (John 5:24)

Now, let me ask you a few more questions.

According to God's holy Word (John 5:24), not your feelings, what kind of life did God just give you? _____

What two words did God say at the beginning of the verse to assure you that He is not lying to you? _____ _____

Are you going to come into eternal judgment? ☐ YES ☐ NO

Have you passed from spiritual death into life? ☐ YES ☐ NO

Friend, you've just been born again. You just became a child of God.

To help you grow in your new Christian life, we would like to send you some Bible study materials. To receive these helpful materials free of charge, e-mail your request to **info@LamplightersUSA.org.**

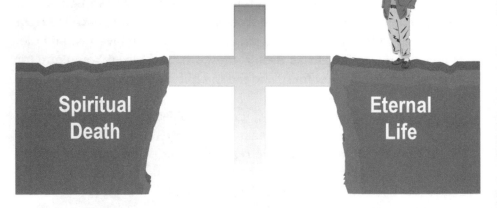

Spiritual
Death

Eternal
Life

APPENDIX

LEVEL 1 (BASIC TRAINING)
STUDENT WORKBOOK

To begin, familiarize yourself with the Lamplighters' *Leadership Training and Development Process* (see graphic on page 122). Notice there are two circles: a smaller, inner circle and a larger, outer circle. The inner circle shows the sequence of weekly meetings beginning with an Open House, followed by an 8–14 week study, and concluding with a clear presentation of the gospel (Final Exam). The outer circle shows the sequence of the Intentional Discipleship training process (Leading Studies, Training Leaders, Multiplying Groups). As participants are transformed by God's Word, they're invited into a discipleship training process that equips them in every aspect of the intentional disciple-making ministry.

The Level 1 training (Basic Training) is *free*, and the training focuses on two key aspects of the training: 1) how to prepare a life-changing Bible study (ST-A-R-T) and 2) how to lead a life-changing Bible study (10 commandments). The training takes approximately 60 minutes to complete, and you complete it as an individual or collectively as a small group (preferred method) by inserting an extra week between the Final Exam and the Open House.

To begin your training, go to www.LamplightersUSA.org to register yourself or your group. A Lamplighters' Certified Trainer will guide you through the entire Level 1 training process. After you have completed the training, you can review as many times as you like.

When you have completed the Level 1 training, please consider completing the Level 2 (Advanced) training. Level 2 training will equip you to reach more people for Christ by learning how to train new leaders and by showing you how to multiply groups. You can register for additional training at www. LamplightersUSA.org.

Intentional Discipleship
Training & Development Process

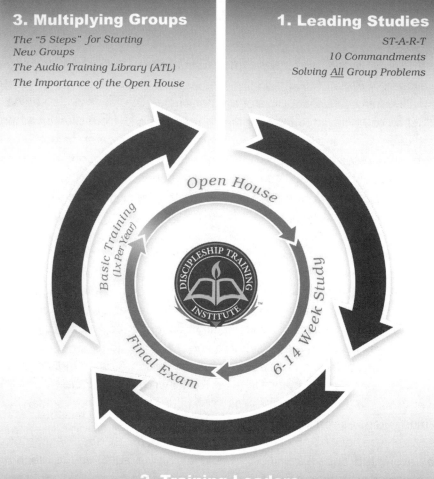

3. Multiplying Groups

The "5 Steps" for Starting New Groups
The Audio Training Library (ATL)
The Importance of the Open House

1. Leading Studies

ST-A-R-T
10 Commandments
Solving All Group Problems

2. Training Leaders

Four-fold ministry of a leader
The Three Diagnostic Questions

The 2P's for recruiting new leaders
The three stages of leadership training

Open House

Basic Training
(1x Per Year)

6-14 Week Study

Final Exam

DISCIPLESHIP TRAINING INSTITUTE

How to Prepare a Life-Changing Bible Study
ST-A-R-T

Step 1: _____ and _____.

    Pray specifically for the group members and yourself as you study God's Word. Ask God (_____) to give each group member a rich time of personal Bible study, and thank (_____) God for giving you a desire to invest in the spiritual advancement of each other.

Step 2: _____ the _____.

    Answer the questions in the weekly lessons without looking at the

_____ _____.

Step 3: _____and _____.

    Review the Leader's Guide, and _____ every truth you missed when you originally did your lesson. Record the answers you missed with a

_____ _____ so you'll know what you missed.

Step 4: _____ _____.

    Calculate the specific amount of time _____ _____ to spend on each question and write the start time next to each one in the

_____ using a _____.

How to Lead a Life-Changing Bible Study

10 COMMANDMENTS

1	2	3
4	5	6
7	8	9
	10	

Lamplighters' 10 Commandments are proven small group leadership principles that have been used successfully to train hundreds of believers to lead life-changing, intentional discipleship Bible studies.

Essential Principles for Leading Intentional Discipleship Bible Studies

1. The 1st Commandment: The _____ Rule.

   The Leader-Trainer should be in the room _____ minutes before the class begins.

2. The 2nd Commandment: The _____-_____ Rule.

   Train the group that it is okay to _____, but they should never be

   _____.

3. The 3rd Commandment: The _____ Rule.

   _____, _____, _____ ask for

   _____ to _____ the _____, _____, and _____

   the questions. The Leader-Trainer, however, should always _____ the

   questions to control the _____ of the study.

4. The 4th Commandment: The ____:____ Rule.

   _____ the Bible study on time and _____ the study on time

   _____ _____. No exceptions!

5. The 5th Commandment: The _____ Rule.

   Train the group participants to _____ on God's Word for answers

   to life's questions.

1	2	3
4 **59:59**	5	6
7	8	9
	10	

6. The 6th Commandment: The _____ Rule.
   Deliberately and progressively _____ _____ participants into the group discussion over a period of time.

7. The 7th Commandment: The _____ _____ Rule.
   _____ the participants to get _____ the answers to the questions, not just _____ or _____ ones.

8. The 8th Commandment: The _____ Rule.
   _____ the group discussion so you _____ the lesson _____ _____ and give each question _____ _____.

9. The 9th Commandment: The _____-_____ Rule.
   Don't let the group members talk about _____ _____ , _____ _____, or _____ _____.

10. The 10th Commandment: The _____ Rule.
    _____ God to change lives, including _____.

Choose your next study from any of the following titles

- John 1-11
- John 12-21
- Acts 1-12
- Acts 13-28
- Romans 1-8
- Romans 9-16
- Galatians
- Ephesians
- Philippians

- Colossians
- 1 & 2 Thessalonians
- 1 Timothy
- 2 Timothy
- Titus/Philemon
- Hebrews
- James
- 1 Peter
- 2 Peter/Jude

Additional Bible studies and sample lessons are available online.

For audio introductions on all Bible studies, visit us online at www.Lamplightersusa.org.

Looking to begin a new group?
The Lamplighters Starter Kit includes:

- 8 James Bible Study Guides
  (students purchase their own books)
- 25 Welcome Booklets
- 25 Table Tents
- 25 Bible Book Locator Bookmarks
- 50 Final Exam Tracts
- 50 Invitation Cards

For a current listing of live and online discipleship training events, or to register for discipleship training, go to www.LamplightersUSA.org/training.

Become a Certified Disciple-Maker or Trainer

Discipleship Training Institute

Certificate of Completion

This is to certify that _____

has successfully completed the requirements of the

_____ course.

_____   _____
Date   President

Training Courses Available:

- Leader-Trainer
- Discipleship Coach
- Discipleship Director
- Certified Trainer (Level 1)

Contact the Discipleship Training Institute for more information (800-507-9516).

The Discipleship Training Institute is a ministry of Lamplighters International.